WOODSTOCK CHRONICLES

WOODSTOCK CHRONICLES

RICHARD HAVERS & RICHARD EVANS

CHARTWELL
BOOKS, INC.

First published in 2009 by

CHARTWELL BOOKS, INC.
A Division of
BOOK SALES, INC.
276 Fifth Avenue Suite 206
New York, New York 10001

ISBN 13: 978-0-7858-2497-8
ISBN 10: 0-7858-2497-9

Compiled, written and designed by
Richard Havers and Richard Evans.

PHOTOGRAPHY

Every effort has been made to trace the copyright holders. Compendium Publishing
apologizes for any unintentional omissions, and would be pleased, if any such case
should arise, to add an appropriate acknowledgement in future editions.

6, 9, 11, 34, 49, 58, 70, 76, 82, 86, 90, 96, 102, 106, 111, 112, 114, 118, 122, 126, 132, 144, 168,
178, 184, 192, 198, 204, 212, 216, 237, 244: © TopFoto/ImageWorks
156, 164, 174: © ImageWorks/TopFoto
108, 223: © TopFoto/UPP
13 (U1191569) , 26 (U1563549), 40 (BE021140), 42 (U1640996), 121 (BE021615),
140 (U1606598), 220 (BE021143), 228: (BE061098) © Bettmann/Corbis
14, 55, 148, 219: © Trinifold Management Ltd.
16 (42-16507367), 225: (42-16504369) © Michael Ochs Archives/Corbis
22 (DZ0033150), 28 (DZ005037), 37 (DZ006526), 38 (DZ006535), 62 (DZ006465),
66 (DZ002863), 75 (DZ006472), 78 (DZ006473), 99 (DZ002152), 104 (42-18308223),
134 (DZ006449), 138 (DZ006448), 147 (DZ006556), 150 (DZ006797), 153 (DZ006552),
154 (DZ006555), 159 (DZ006616), 160 (DZ006489), 187 (DZ006457), 190 (DZ006454),
195 (DZ006467), 206/7 (DZ002606), 208 (DZ006469), 240 (DZ006479), 252 (DZ005441) :
© Henry Diltz/Corbis
30 (TS002696), 68 (TS001002), 137: (TS001356) © Ted Streshinsky/Corbis
234: (BE064837) © Corbis
53: (DWF15-527593) © Douglas Kent Hall/ZUMA/Corbis
72: (HU046878) © Hulton-Deutsch Collection/Corbis
227: (20563338) © James Andanson/Apis/Sygma/Corbis
230: (DWF15-527579) © Douglas Kent Hall/ZUMA/Corbis
51: © Michael Ochs Archives/Getty Images
57: © Richard Evans
92: © Time & Life Pictures/Getty Images
115 (Bottom right): © Phil Beards and John Morawski/
courtesy of www.pappalardi.com
131, 172, 202: © Getty Images
182: © James Summaria: Arena Images
233: © Jan Olafsson: Arena Images

CONTENTS

By the Time We Got To Woodstock 8

Festivals Before Woodstock 12

Festival Timeline 18

From the Summer of Love to Woodstock 24

The Idea for Woodstock 32

Getting to Woodstock 40

Woodstock Voices 44

The Original Running Order 48

The Bands 50

The Wages of Woodstock 56

WOODSTOCK DAY ONE: 15 August 1969 60

Richie Havens 62

Sweetwater 64

Bert Sommer 65

Tim Hardin 66

Ravi Shanker 68

Melanie 72

Arlo Guthrie 74

Joan Baez 78

WOODSTOCK DAY TWO: 16 August 1969 84

Quill 88

Country Joe McDonald 89

Santana 92

John Sebastian 98

The Keef Hartley Band 100

The Incredible String Band 104

Canned Heat 108

Mountain 114

The Grateful Dead 120

Creedence Clearwater Revival 128

Janis Joplin 134

Sly & The Family Stone 140

The Who 146

Jefferson Airplane 158

WOODSTOCK DAY THREE: 17 August 1969 166

Joe Cocker 170

Country Joe & The Fish 176

Ten Years After 180

The Band 186

Johnny Winter 194

Blood, Sweat & Tears 200

Crosby, Stills, Nash & Young 206

The Paul Butterfield Blues Band 214

Sha Na Na 218

Jimi Hendrix 220

Aftermath 238

Woodstock, The Song 239

The Once & Future Festival 242

Woodstock, The Albums 246

Woodstock, The Movie 248

Woodstock 94 250

Index 254

15-17 AUGUST 1969

BY THE TIME WE GOT TO WOODSTOCK

NO ONE EVER DID GET TO Woodstock for a festival; at least the place where it was originally going to be held. Instead they got to go to some alfalfa fields near Bethel – population 3,900; it's a place about a hundred miles north of New York City and 60 miles to the southwest of the town of Woodstock. The actual site of the Woodstock Aquarian Music and Art Fair, as we all now know, was Max Yasgur's 660-acre dairy farm in White Lake. For a brief period in between deciding to have a festival at Woodstock and settling on Bethel it was going to be in a place named Wallkill. The organizers decided to stick with their original name simply because it played to their anticipated audience through a resonance to the artistic community who lived in Woodstock. It was probably just as well, somehow the Bethel Festival just doesn't sound right.

"We didn't know it was going to be a cultural landmark." ~ Fito de la Parra of Canned Heat

No-one of course knew just how significant an event in the history of the 20th-Century the festival was to be. What made Woodstock such a cultural landmark? Who knows – exactly? On the one hand it's easy to see why; well over half a million people turned up. Such a large crowd had never, ever, attended a concert or music event; it's the major reason why Woodstock became such a 'happening.'

The festival was extremely peaceful, especially so given the size of the crowd and some of what they had to endure. There were rainstorms, the frustrations of sometimes waiting hours for anything to happen, there were food shortages, water shortages, but there seemed to be no shortage of drugs. Perhaps most of all it was the sheer scale of the logistics associated with such a huge event, run by people with little or no experience of such things, that made it so

amazing. The fact is no-one in the world had any real experience of organizing an event on such a scale. Two people died, one it is thought from a heroin overdose, the other was run over by a tractor while he slept beneath its wheels. More people die in a town or city of half a million in any given three-day period; then again nobody at Woodstock was likely to die of old age.

One thing's for sure, Woodstock's reputation wasn't all down to the music. However, for various reasons, including the need to sleep and the need to travel back home for work, many of the half-million people who were there on Sunday morning probably missed some of the best of the music, because it happened on Monday morning.

The fact is Woodstock was a cultural landmark waiting to happen – one that needed to happen. The sixties had been building towards it; the counterculture, the young, those against the war and those just wanting to break free from an older generation who had been through World War II, one that couldn't understand why their kids didn't support American troops in Vietnam. Finally the planets aligned and despite the best, and sometimes the worst efforts of those involved in Woodstock's organization, it came to pass.

"History is written by the victors."
~ Sir Winston Churchill

Was Winston Churchill really the first to say it? Some doubt it, but whatever the case it's now been

attributed to him. The fact is there were many winners at Woodstock. There were the artists, especially those who featured in the movie. There were the people who took the risk to film the festival, and those that organized it. They are the ones who have largely written the history. When the film was shown in cinemas across the world millions of young people said to themselves and to their friends, "I wish I'd been there." Ever afterwards festivals have tried to emulate Woodstock; even The Rolling Stones tried to create their own Woodstock out West at the Altamont Racetrack, an event that so tragically ended with murder and the death of the sixties dream. It proved just how thin the line between glory or failure can be.

No one at Woodstock kept notes, because no one thought it was that important. Back then popular culture somehow didn't seem to be as important as we've come to think of it today. In the immediate aftermath there didn't even seem to be that much hoop-la about the whole affair. It's only as the telescope of history has gradually been extended that the cultural significance of Woodstock has been truly recognized.

This is a story of the Woodstock Festival…

FESTIVALS BEFORE WOODSTOCK

WOODSTOCK WAS FAR FROM the first rock festival and as we know now a long way from the last, yet every festival organizer ever since has secretly wanted to match its success. It was the jazz festivals at Newport in the Fifties that were the original outdoor festivals from which music festivals throughout the Sixties, before Woodstock, took their inspiration. Even in England there were small-scale open-air events that might just have passed for festivals, and these too were organised by jazz enthusiasts. The size and scale of festivals have always been determined by technology, particularly the P.A. system allowing the audience to be able to hear the performers at an acceptable volume.

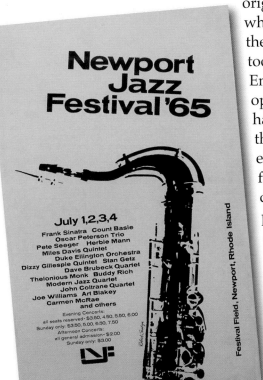

Newport Jazz Festival '65

July 1,2,3,4

Frank Sinatra   Count Basie
Oscar Peterson Trio
Pete Seeger   Herbie Mann
Miles Davis Quintet
Duke Ellington Orchestra
Dizzy Gillespie Quintet   Stan Getz
Dave Brubeck Quartet
Thelonious Monk   Buddy Rich
Modern Jazz Quartet
John Coltrane Quartet
Joe Williams   Art Blakey
Carmen McRae
and others

Evening Concerts:
all seats reserved- $3.50, 4.50, 5.50, 6.00
Sunday only: $3.50, 5.00, 6.50, 7.50
Afternoon Concerts:
all general admission- $2.00
Sunday only: $3.00

Festival Field, Newport, Rhode Island

THE NEWPORT JAZZ FESTIVAL

Jazz impresario George Wein established the Newport Jazz Festival in 1954 in Newport, Rhode Island; for many this was the first open-air festival of the modern era and was a template for many of the festivals that followed. The first one, in July 1954, was at the old open-air casino and around 6,000 people turned up for the opening night. The following year, after the owners of the casino refused permission for it to be held there, Louis and Elaine Lorillard bought an old property named Belacourt on Bellevue Avenue and financed the festival. The festival continued to grow but after a riot at the 1971 event it moved to New York City the following year, but returned in 1981 when it was held in both Newport and New York City.

THE NATIONAL JAZZ & BLUES FESTIVAL

The longest-running of the British festivals was established in 1961 when the National Jazz Federation decided to set up a very British version of Newport. The first festival took place in Richmond, to the west of London, in August 1961 and was almost entirely made up of British jazz, with Chris Barber the most well-known name on the bill. This was the template for many of the festivals that followed in Britain and as it gradually became more blues than jazz and then more rock than blues it attracted more and more people.

FANTASY FAIRE & MAGIC MOUNTAIN MUSIC FESTIVAL AND MONTEREY POP FESTIVAL

The first real American rock festival was held at Mount Tamalpais in California on the weekend of 10-11 June 1967. Billed as the Fantasy Faire & Magic Mountain Music Festival it had an eclectic mix of performers ranging from Jefferson Airplane, The

The great Jimmy Rushing singing at the Newport Jazz Festival, 3 July 1959

Doors, Country Joe & The Fish and The Byrds to Dionne Warwick and Smokey Robinson. 15,000 people showed up for what was a non-profit event that cost just $2 to get in with all profits going to a nearby child care center.

While the Fantasy Faire was first, Monterey is the festival that everyone remembers. With a line-up that read like a who's who in pop music – as in short for popular. Otis Redding got his first exposure to a rock audience and others on the bill included The Mamas & The Papas, Jimi Hendrix, The Who, Janis Joplin and Ravi Shankar. Captured on film it did much to enhance its reputation and the myth.

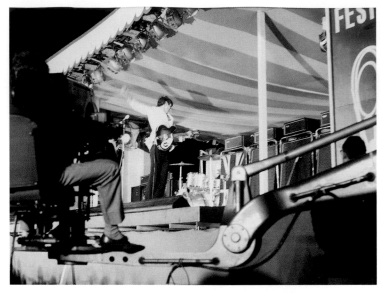

The Who at the 5th National Jazz & Blues Festival in Richmond, England, 1965

1968 NEWPORT POP FESTIVAL

This was the first music festival to attract over 100,000 paying members of the public. It was staged at the Orange County Fairgrounds at Costa Mesa, California over the weekend of 3-4 August 1968. Held in a large flat dusty field it was like Woodstock faced with sanitation and water shortages from early on the first day of the festival, with organizers just not equipped or experienced to stage such an event. City official came to the rescue with portable toilets and water tanks. Among those appearing were Jefferson Airplane, Country Joe &The Fish, The Grateful Dead, The Chambers Brothers, The Electric Flag, Sonny & Cher, Quicksilver Messenger Service, The Byrds and the enigmatic Tiny Tim. At $5.50 per day this was not considered one of the great festival bargains, especially given the conditions.

FESTIVAL BRITAIN

As the Jazz & Blues Festival developed it was joined by other events that ranged from the free concerts in Hyde Park, London to the first Isle of Wight festival, which starred Jefferson Airplane. The Hyde Park events were small to begin with, very hippie-esque and low key, but all the better for it. The first line-up was Pink Floyd, Jethro Tull, Tyrannosaurus Rex and the ubiquitous U.K. festival artist – Roy Harper. There was also a small-scale festival at Woburn, which was headlined by Jimi Hendrix.

FESTIVALS IN 1969

It could be argued that 1969 was THE year of the festivals. Across North America and Britain festivals seemed to be happening somewhere almost every weekend in the summer. The two earliest festivals that summer were in Canada, including the Aldergrove Beach Rock Festival that bizarrely starred The New Vaudeville Band and Guitar Shorty. In Britain the first Hyde Park show starred Blind Faith, with Richie Havens opening proceedings in front of 120,000 people.

Newport '69 was bigger than its predecessor, this time taking place at Northridge at the Devonshire Downs Racetrack. Over 150,000 people showed up to another one of those eclectic Sixties line-ups with Jimi Hendrix receiving top billing at the three-day festival held over the weekend of 20 – 22 June. Gangs crashed the gates by the thousands, and threw sticks, bottles and rocks at the police. Other artists at the festival included Albert King, Joe Cocker, Spirit, Albert Collins, Love, Steppenwolf, Creedence Clearwater Revival, Flock, Johnny Winter, The Byrds, The Rascals and Three Dog Night. On the same weekend in Toronto, a festival for 50,000 people featured The Band, Canada's own Steppenwolf and Chuck Berry.

The following weekend Denver got in on the act and played host to 50,000 fans to watch Poco, Creedence Clearwater Revival, Joe Cocker and the very last gig by the Jimi Hendrix Experience; gate-crashers lobbed firecrackers, bottles and debris at the police and the police threw tear gas. The same weekend in England, the Bath Festival of Blues was held. Top of the bill was Fleetwood Mac, supported by John Mayall, Ten Years After, Led Zeppelin, The Nice and Keef Hartley, who was well down the bill.

The first weekend in July the Atlanta Pop Festival attracted 140,000 and passed off with no violence or trouble as the crowd watched Creedence Clearwater

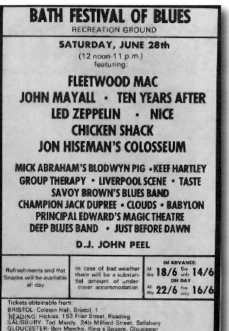

Revival, Led Zeppelin, Blood Sweat & Tears and Ten Wheel Drive among a packed two-day bill. On Saturday 5 July in London's Hyde Park The Rolling Stones were staging their now famous free concert for anything from 250,000 to 500,000 people – no one counted.

Two weeks later, at the Newport Folk Festival Joni Mitchell and James Taylor met for the first time as they performed on a bill that included Richie Havens. The next weekend in Seattle, The Doors, Led Zeppelin and Bo Diddley among others performed for 70,000 people over the course of the three-day festival.

Atlantic City during the first weekend in August was the scene for the first New York area festival when 110,000 fans turned up to see Procol Harum, Little Richard, Santana, Jefferson Airplane and almost inevitably Creedence Clearwater Revival. A week later at a horse-racing track at Plumpton in southern England, the National Jazz & Blues Festival was an almost totally rock-orientated bill. On the Friday night Pink Floyd topped the bill, Saturday had The Who, Yes and Chicken Shack, while Sunday featured The Nice, Keef Hartley, Pentangle and Family.

And then it was Woodstock…

Joan Baez and her sister Mimi Farina performing at the 1967 Newport Folk Festival

FESTIVAL TIMELINE

That Newport Jazz (1964)

1954 NEWPORT JAZZ FESTIVAL
Dizzy Gillespie, Oscar Peterson, Gerry Mulligan, George Shearing, Erroll Garner.

1955 NEWPORT JAZZ FESTIVAL
Miles Davis, Louis Armstrong, The Modern Jazz Quartet, Woody Herman, Dave Brubeck.

1956 NEWPORT JAZZ FESTIVAL
Duke Ellington's Orchestra.

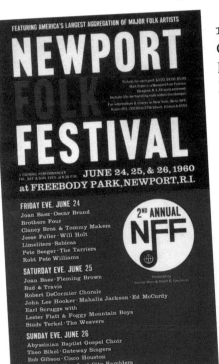

1957 NEWPORT JAZZ FESTIVAL
Gerry Mulligan, Count Basie and Dave Brubeck, Erroll Garner, Ella Fitzgerald.

1958 NEWPORT JAZZ FESTIVAL
Miles Davis & Thelonious Monk, Ella Fitzgerald, Billie Holiday.

1959 NEWPORT FOLK FESTIVAL
The first folk festival featuring Joan Baez, Pete Seeger, Sonny Terry & Brownie McGhee.

1960 NEWPORT JAZZ FESTIVAL
Muddy Waters, Nina Simone.

1960 NEWPORT FOLK FESTIVAL
Pete Seeger, Lester Flatt & Earl Scruggs.

1961 NEWPORT JAZZ FESTIVAL
Cannonball Adderley, Dave Brubeck.

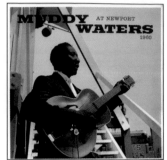

Muddy Waters at Newport (1960)

1961 THE NATIONAL JAZZ & BLUES FESTIVAL
Richmond, England, 26-27 August
Chris Barber, Johnny Dankworth.

1962 NEWPORT JAZZ FESTIVAL
Oscar Peterson Trio, Duke Ellington Orchestra, Count Basie Orchestra and Jimmy Rushing.

1962 THE NATIONAL JAZZ & BLUES FESTIVAL
Richmond, England, 28-29 July
Chris Barber, Johnny Dankworth.

1963 NEWPORT JAZZ FESTIVAL
Miles Davis & Thelonious Monk.

1963 NEWPORT FOLK FESTIVAL
Bob Dylan, Joan Baez, Tom Paxton, Ewan MacColl, John Lee Hooker, Rev. Gary Davis.

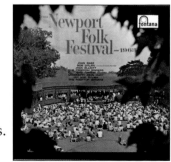

Newport Folk Festival (1963)

1963 THE NATIONAL JAZZ & BLUES FESTIVAL *Richmond, England, 10-11 August* Chris Barber, Acker Bilk, The Rolling Stones.

1964 THE NATIONAL JAZZ & BLUES FESTIVAL *Richmond, England, 7-9 August* The Rolling Stones, Memphis Slim, The Yardbirds (with Eric Clapton), Chris Barber.

1964 NEWPORT FOLK FESTIVAL Bob Dylan, Joan Baez, Fred MacDowell, Skip James, Jose Feliciano, Phil Ochs, Koerner, Ray & Glover.

1965 THE NATIONAL JAZZ & BLUES FESTIVAL *Richmond, England, 6-8 August*

The Who, Chris Barber, The Moody Blues, The Animals, The Steampacket with Rod Stewart, Julie Driscoll and The Brian Auger Trinity.

1965 NEWPORT FOLK FESTIVAL The 'electric' Bob Dylan, The Paul Butterfield Blues Band, Son House, The Chambers Brothers.

1966 THE NATIONAL JAZZ & BLUES FESTIVAL *Windsor, England, 29-31 July* The Who, Chris Barber, Cream, The Move, Small Faces.

1966 NEWPORT FOLK FESTIVAL Tim Hardin, Ramblin' Jack Elliott, Phil Ochs, Son House.

1967 FANTASY FAIRE & MAGIC MOUNTAIN MUSIC FESTIVAL *Mount Tamalpais, California* Jefferson Airplane, The Doors, The Byrds, Canned Heat, Country Joe & The Fish.

1967 NEWPORT FOLK FESTIVAL Arlo Guthrie, Muddy Waters, Sister Rosetta Tharpe, The Staples Singers.

1967 THE NATIONAL JAZZ & BLUES FESTIVAL *Windsor, England, 11-13 August* Jeff Beck, The Nice, Cream, The Move, Small Faces, Fleetwood Mac.

1967 MONTEREY INTERNATIONAL POP FESTIVAL *16-16 June 1967* The Who, Jimi Hendrix, Janis Joplin, Country Joe & The Fish, Jefferson Airplane, Grateful Dead, Buffalo Springfield, Ravi Shankar.

Ravi Shankar Live at the Monterey Pop Festival (1967)

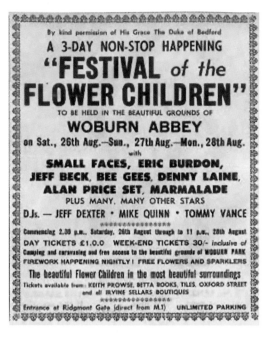

1967 FESTIVAL OF FLOWER CHILDREN
Woburn Abbey, England, 26-28 August
Small Faces, Eric Burdon, Jeff Beck, The Bee Gees, Denny Laine, The Alan Price Set, Marmalade.

1968 HYDE PARK
London, 29 June
Pink Floyd, Jethro Tull, Tyrannosaurus Rex.

1968 HYDE PARK
London, 27 July
Traffic, Nice, Pretty Things.

1968 NEWPORT FOLK FESTIVAL
Maria Maldaur, Junior Wells & Buddy Guy, Bill Monroe & his Bluegrass Boys.

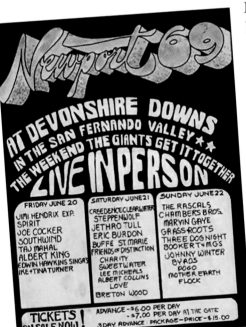

1968 THE NATIONAL JAZZ & BLUES FESTIVAL
Sunbury, England, 9-11 August
The Herd, Jerry Lee Lewis, Joe Cocker, Ten Years After, Traffic, Jethro Tull.

1968 HYDE PARK
London, 24 August
Family, Fleetwood Mac, Ten Years After.

1968 HYDE PARK *London, 28 September*
The Move, Strawbs, Roy Harper.

1968 WOBURN MUSIC FESTIVAL
Bedfordshire, England, 6-7 July
Jimi Hendrix, Fleetwood Mac.

1968 NEWPORT POP FESTIVAL
Costa Mesa, California
Jefferson Airplane, Canned Heat, The Paul Butterfield Blues Band, The Byrds, Iron Butterfly, Grateful Dead, Quicksilver Messenger Service.

1968 ISLE OF WIGHT FESTIVAL
Godshill, Isle of Wight, England, 31 August-1 September
Jefferson Airplane, The Crazy World of Arthur Brown, Fairport Convention, Aynsley Dunbar Retaliation, Pretty Things.

1969 ALDERGROVE BEACH ROCK FESTIVAL *British Columbia, Canada*
The New Vaudeville Band, Guitar Shorty, Valdy, The Mike Beddoes Blues Band.

1969 HYDE PARK *London, 7 June*
Blind Faith, Richie Havens, Donovan.

1969 NEWPORT '69 FESTIVAL
Devonshire Downs, California, 20-22 June
Jimi Hendrix, Creedence Clearwater Revival, Jethro

Tull, Marvin Gaye, Johnny Winter, Sweetwater.

1969 TORONTO FESTIVAL *22 June*
Steppenwolf, The Band, Procol Harum, Blood Sweat & Tears, Chuck Berry.

1969 DENVER POP FESTIVAL *27-29 June*
Jimi Hendrix, Johnny Winter, Creedence Clearwater Revival, Joe Cocker, The Mothers of Invention.

1969 BATH FESTIVAL OF BLUES
Bath, England, 28 June
Led Zeppelin, The Nice, Fleetwood Mac, Ten Years After, John Mayall's Bluesbreakers.

1969 ATLANTA POP FESTIVAL *4-5 July*
Led Zeppelin, Joe Cocker, Janis Joplin, Blood Sweat & Tears, Delaney & Bonnie.

1969 HYDE PARK
London, 5 July
The Rolling Stones, King Crimson.

1969 NEWPORT FOLK FESTIVAL *July 19-20*
Richie Havens, James Taylor, Joni Mitchell, Arlo Guthrie, Pentangle.

1969 THE SEATTLE POP FESTIVAL
Woodinville, Washington, 25-27 July
The Doors, Tim Buckley, Chuck Berry, Led Zeppelin, Vanilla Fudge, The Byrds, Chicago Transit Authority, Spirit.

1969 ATLANTIC CITY POP FESTIVAL *August 1-3*
Jefferson Airplane, Creedence Clearwater Revival, Santana, BB King, Joe Cocker, Janis Joplin.

1969 THE NATIONAL JAZZ & BLUES FESTIVAL
Plumpton, England, 8-10 August (Originally billed as West Drayton, near Heathrow Airport)
Pink Floyd, Soft Machine, The Who, Yes, The Nice, Keef Hartley, King Crimson, Chris Barber, John Mayall's Bluesbreakers, Donovan, The Idle Race.

The Human Be-In at Golden Gate Park, San Francisco, 14 January 1967. L to R: Allen Ginsberg, Maretta Greer, Gary Synder and Michael Bowen

FROM THE SUMMER OF

FOR SOME, 1967's SUMMER OF LOVE had its origins on a mid-January day in San Francisco's Golden Gate Park; for others, and especially those gathered at the Polo Grounds, this was the last day of the true hippies. But there's no question that for many people the ideals and aspirations of those involved in the Woodstock Festival there was a direct line connecting 14 January 1967 to that momentous weekend in the middle of August 1969.

"A union of love and activism previously separated by categorical dogma and label mongering will finally occur ecstatically when Berkeley political activists and hip community and San Francisco's spiritual generation and contingents from the emerging revolutionary generation all over California meet for a Gathering of the Tribes for a Human Be-In at the Polo Fields in Golden Gate Park." ~ The Human Be-In press release

The hippie movement that had developed from the hipsters, those involved in liberal politics, students from Berkeley and Stanford, along with the flotsam and jetsam of a youth culture attracted to the radical and very different lifestyles than those affected by the post-war consumer society of their parents, all helped to create the environment in which the Human Be-In came about. It was organized by Michael Bowen, an

LOVE TO WOODSTOCK

artist and activist who was a central figure in the Haight-Ashbury area of San Francisco (Haight and Ashbury is an intersection of two streets that gave the area its name – a name that resonates around the world). Bowen created a poster for the Be-In and gathered others around him to speak at the event, including Timothy Leary, beat poets Allen Ginsberg and Gary Snyder, and Richard Alpert who later became spiritual teacher Baba Ram Dass. Also there was Owsley Stanley, the underground's chief chemist, who provided industrial amounts of LSD to the crowd of 20,000 or so that turned up to turn on.

As well as listening to the speeches at the Gathering of Love, the crowd were entertained by the cream of the San Francisco bands – The Grateful Dead, Jefferson Airplane, Big Brother & The Holding Company and Quicksilver Messenger Service. At around 5:00pm as the light was just starting to fade, Ginsberg led everyone in the chanting of "Om Sri Maitreya" after which everyone started to clear up their collective rubbish; many headed for the beach to watch the sun go down.

As with many such events in history, those commenting on them have made a habit of changing some of the key facts. The numbers at the Be-In have swelled to 100,000 according to many newspaper articles written in the last 20 years. There was no violence and no police according to some; that is unless you count the guy that was beaten up in front of a photographer by the 'security'-minded Hells Angels. The legend of the hippie idyll was nurtured and before long more people were attracted to San Francisco, with them came increasing problems and a tarnishing of the dream.

Five months later at the Monterey County Fairgrounds, over the middle weekend of June, the Monterey Pop Festival attracted around 200,000 people, although not all at the same time, to what was the first major rock festival in America. It was organized by Lou Adler, John Phillips of The Mamas & The Papas and Derek Taylor, the former Beatles' publicist and their ambition was to create an event that was multi-cultural, multi-national and multi-styled in the music that was performed. It was truly a first and it can be

"Turn on, tune in, drop out." ~ Timothy Leary

considered the premier event of the Summer of Love; one at which everything seemed to work and about which nothing bad has ever been written.

In particular Monterey helped launch the careers of many performers, catapulting them from local, or relative obscurity, into the forefront of American and worldwide awareness. Today it's easy to forget that before Monterey Jimi Hendrix had not had a hit record in America. Neither had The Who managed to get a record into the *Billboard* Top 20 and only one of their four minor hits had got higher than No. 51; nor was Otis Redding very well known among white audiences. Rolling Stone Brian Jones was there; according to one report he was "…in a mind-shattering gold-lame coat festooned with beads, crystal swastika and lace, looked like a kind of unofficial King of the Festival" Brian Jones was the king of hippie-chic.

George Harrison with ex-Beatles publicist Derek Taylor in Golden Gate Park, San Francisco, 7 August 1967

" This is really a great scene here. All the kids are so nice. The people are so polite and just come up and talk to me and say they like the way I'm dressed." ~ Brian Jones

Press attention from around the world, and particularly the music press, alerted fans to what was happening, but it wasn't until the end of 1968 that people were able to see the documentary made by D.A. Pennebaker – for most people this was the first time that they actually saw Jimi Hendrix set fire to his Stratocaster. It has not had the effect of the

Woodstock movie, which could be put down to the fact that the commercial precepts were less well developed at this point. Big business had not cottoned onto the money-making potential of a 'bunch of hippies.'

The Beatles released *Sgt Pepper's Lonely Hearts Club Band* two weeks before Monterey took place, and just

"I was with Brian for the Monterey Pop Festival and we took acid in a tepee." ~ Dennis Hopper

as the festival became the template for many that followed, the Fab Four's album signaled a new way of doing things on record; music was no longer Pop, and while it was not quite Rock, it was something that even intelligent people listened to. Perhaps it might even be art. *Sgt Pepper's* was made No. 1 in *Rolling Stone*'s list of the 500 Greatest Albums of All Time. Significantly a large number of albums released between the Human Be-In and Woodstock are on that list; many of them by artists that appeared at either Monterey or Woodstock, or both. Jimi Hendrix's *Are You Experienced*, The Band's *Music from Big Pink*, Creedence Clearwater Revival's *Green River* and The Who's *Tommy* to name just a few.

By October 1967 things were changing in San Francisco where the Diggers, the radical improv theatre group, held a 'Death of Hippie' celebration, a mock funeral no less. An empty, open coffin was wheeled down Haight Street and thousands of people threw beads, strands of their long hair, and even tabs of LSD into it. But in the rest of the world people were beginning to turn on to the commercial possibilities of flower power, the over-the-counter culture, and all things hippie.

MONTEREY INTERNATIONAL POP FESTIVAL

JUNE 16·17·18

MONTEREY COUNTY FAIRGROUNDS, MONTEREY, CALIF.

In America and Britain 1968 dawned with the prescient 'Hello Goodbye'; the Beatles at No. 1 seemed to say it all. The charts were full of records that heralded something very different from the days when there seemed to be little other than discs by boring men named Bobby. Even The Doors made No. 1 in America; The Rascals topped the charts singing about "People everywhere just wanna be free." Freedom was the new black, when black clothes were the last things on anyone's mind; these were the days of the rainbow people, when everything was kaleidoscopic.

This was the new world order where the young were able to really make things happen; 'The Man' was no longer an impediment to making dreams come true, whether your dreams were something cerebral or just about making money.

Interestingly, the Hells Angels provided security for the Human Be-In and their presence would be felt at what was arguably the real funeral of the hippie movement in the eyes of America and the world. Altamont, less than four months after Woodstock, was almost literally, and certainly metaphorically, the end of the Sixties.

Janis Joplin with Big Brother & the Holding Company on stage at the Monterey Pop Festival, 17 June 1967

THE IDEA FOR WOODSTOCK

THE WOODSTOCK FESTIVAL had its genesis back in March 1968 thanks to two wannabe entrepreneurs putting an advert in the *New York Times* and the *Wall Street Journal*.

The 'young men' were John Roberts and Joel Rosenman; among the 7,000 replies was an idea for bicycles on skis, biodegradable golf balls and a whole lot more 'ideas' that would have probably landed them in prison. John, who was 23 and Joel, 24, also had an idea of their own – a TV sitcom about two well-heeled young men with unlimited funds, and crucially no brains, on the loose in New York City. It was only semi-autobiographical.

John Roberts was the man with the money; he was heir to the Block Drug Company fortune on his father's side and a toothpaste manufacturing fortune on his mother's. He had met Joel Rosenman, who had been playing guitar in a lounge band, on a golf course. Rosenman was by far the hipper of the two, although his background was equally as proper, if not quite as rich; his father was a Long Island orthodontist and Joel was a Yale Law School graduate.

Two men from the complete opposite side of the tracks to Roberts and Rosenman had got to know each other through their shared love of music and the fact that they had both grown up in the Queens district of New York City. Arthur Kornfield was 25 years old in late 1968, the son of a New York policeman and already something of a success story at Capitol Records where he was a Vice-President and a veteran composer of a whole batch of singles including 'I'm The Pied Piper' for a band called The Changin' Times – Artie was also half of The Changin' Times. He also co-wrote Jan & Dean's prophetic, 'Dead Man's Curve' and the wonderful 'The Rain, The Park & Other Things' for The Cowsills. By December 1968 he had an office and a secretary; one day she buzzed Artie to say a guy named Michael Lang was there to see him. He didn't know Lang, but saw him because he also came from Queens.

Michael, who was 23, was managing a group named The Train who he was anxious for Artie to sign. Lang, a curly-haired small guy with a smile to die for, had been involved in producing the two-day Miami Pop Festival, where 40,000 people had shown

up making it one of the biggest events of its kind. While Artie appeared the straighter of the two, he was not averse to smoking a joint in his office and the two quickly became firm friends; so much so that Lang, who rented a room out in Woodstock, would often crash at Artie and his wife's apartment in the city when he missed the last bus home.

A discussion that the two of them kept coming back to was the idea of running their own festival, where 100,000 might show up; Artie's wife Linda thought 10,000 was the more likely number. Eventually they decided to do something about it.

and agents in order to sign the right acts to appear, as well as creating the right vibe among the prospective audience was essential. When a copywriter friend came up with the notion of 'Three Days of Peace and Music' they all knew they were on to something. The four of them had started out with the idea of the zodiac references of an 'Aquarian Exposition' and decided the two played well together; they needed to begin running adverts for the event in the press, they also schmoozed the writers from *Rolling Stone* and *Village Voice* to accentuate their hip credentials for organizing the festival.

"To get the contracts, we had to have the credibility, and to get the credibility, we had to have the contracts." ~ Joel Rosenman

Despite having never seen Roberts' and Rosenman's advert, the four of them met in February 1969. John and Joel were involved in the funding of a recording studio and Artie and Michael were anxious for them to do something similar for them or to get involved in some way. At their first meeting Artie did most of the talking, whereas Michael did a good deal of smiling and dissemination of good vibes, but it worked and in March the four young guys started Woodstock Ventures with an initial capital of $250,000; they each held a 25% share.

They established an office on 57th Street and set about making things happen – the event started out as an outdoor festival for 50,000 people. Woodstock Ventures leased some land in Wallkill in upstate New York; it was at the 300-acre Mills Industrial Park, which offered great access to the freeways and, very importantly, water and electricity already on the site. Its one drawback according to Lang was that it lacked the ambience necessary for what he wanted to put on, but for now this was all they had.

Meanwhile, getting things moving with managers

Getting the right bands to commit was proving a little problematical, as Woodstock Ventures had no track record in promoting concerts. They got around this small detail by offering contracts at vastly inflated rates – often doubling a band's normal paycheck for a show. Soon bands were lining up to be signed.

Having got the words right they set about getting the visuals down and graphic artist Arnold Skolnick created the now famous poster; as emblematic of the Sixties as any image. While things were moving well on the artistic front, by June there were signs that all was not well with the town of Wallkill; rumblings in the community about the desirability of having a 'bunch of hippies' take over the place were making things difficult. Finally, at a meeting on 15 July 1969, to the residents' delight The Wallkill Zoning Board of Appeals banned the Woodstock Festival from taking place in their town. It was a disaster … or was it?

Lang in particular was glad, as he never wanted to hold the festival there in any event; the very public row paid dividends in an unexpected manner. Elliot

Festival organisers John Roberts, Joel Rosenman and Michael Lang

Tiber, the proprietor of Tiber's White Lake resort, read the news and saw this as the opportunity to save his struggling hotel complex. He knew he had something vital to the success of the venture, a permit to run a music festival from the town of Bethel. Tiber got Lang on the phone and the next day the rock entrepreneur was in his car on his way to White Lake; when he got there his first reaction was disappointment; the 15-acre boggy site was far from big enough. This is where Max Yasgur makes his triumphal entry, or more to the point, Tiber suggests they go and see the dairy farmer who owned around 600 acres that would be perfect. Initially Yasgur had been sceptical on the phone with Tiber – he was used

Everything from drugs to sex frightened the Bethel residents about the upcoming festival, but slowly, although not too slowly as time was running out, and surely, things started to fall into place. At least one local resident seems to have offered to 'make things happen' for a one time pay-off of $10,000, although whether this or other monies ever got paid, no one is quite sure. Finally, in late July Woodstock Ventures got their permit and despite the many objectors there were some in Bethel and the surrounding area that were relieved, believing it was just the boost their ailing economy needed. Nevertheless, over 800 out of Bethel's almost-4,000 residents signed a petition against the festival.

"Buy No Milk. Stop Max's Hippy Music Festival." ~ Signs in Bethel

to his friend's failing festival schemes – but eventually he agreed to meet Lang, who drove over to the now-famous sloping site that was an almost perfect setting for a huge concert.

Yasgur, before taking over his family's dairy farm in the 1940s, had gone to New York University where he studied real estate law. He eventually bought the Bethel site in order to expand his herd and business into what was, by 1969, the largest milk producer in Sullivan County. He was no fool and by the time the rest of the Woodstock Ventures team headed out to the country from Manhattan he was prepared to drive a hard bargain. There was also the issue of dealing with the people who lived in Bethel, who broadly shared the same views as the Wallkill residents. Central to this was the Woodstock Ventures position of never saying there would be more than 50,000 people showing up for the weekend – despite their certainty that there would be. Mr. Yasgur, of course, was towing the party line, as he wanted to get the $75,000 rental fee, while Elliot Tiber just wanted to fill his 80 rooms.

However, by early August, and not before time, work was underway at the site, albeit a little on the laid-back side. As can be seen in the movie, things moved at a fairly relaxed pace with none of the high tech equipment on hand that is used at today's rock shows to build the stage and create a proper concert environment; Woodstock relied on old-fashioned manpower. Rosenman and Roberts had persuaded Michael Wadleigh to make a documentary of the festival; Wadleigh had a very low estimate of his chances of it making any money or being critically appreciated. Two days before the festival started Artie Kornfield sold the film rights to Warner Bros. for $100,000; a real deal.

By Thursday 14 August, there were around 25,000 people on the Woodstock site – it showed all the signs of becoming a (rather large) hippie commune. Wavy Gravy and The Hog Farmers had built kitchens and recruited people as security guards; they even had a secret password – "I forget." By Friday morning Bethel was heaving with hippies; some were camped in people's gardens while others

"Wavy Gravy is the illegitimate son of Harpo Marx and Mother Teresa."
~ Paul Krassner, author and comedian

just slept in their cars, unable to move for the crush of traffic making its way to the site. Up at the site there was one very important moneymaking essential that was not in place. According to Michael Lang, "Tickets were being handled over in the office. I just assumed that they were handling the booths, but they were never put in place." No money could be taken at the gate because there was nowhere to take it and no one to collect it.

Shortly after breakfast on Friday, three school buses full of around one hundred New York City police officers arrived; they were to handle the real security and were being paid $50 a day. However, the Police Department was unhappy with their moonlighting and a message was received demanding that they all return. In the end most stayed and worked under assumed names, there were a lot of Disney characters employed that weekend, with their pay increased to $90 a day.

Everything was in place for a great festival, even if the economics were going to be a little stretched without the gate money. An awful lot of $18 tickets had been pre-sold, therefore, it was possibly assumed, guaranteeing enough money to cover the spiraling costs of the artists ($180,000), the site costs ($100,000) and the plethora of costs associated with building the stage and other production money. Plus the $10,000 that Abbie Hoffman had extracted from Rosenman and Lang in order not "to bring this whole thing down".

'Woodstock - 3 Days of Peace and Music' was about to begin. All they needed were some artists to perform.

Wavy Gravy (left) and members of the Hog Farm Collective, who organized the free kitchen and the Freak Out tent

GETTING TO WOODSTOCK

THE PUBLIC AND THE PERFORMERS at Woodstock shared a common problem, because getting to the festival site, whether you wanted to watch or to perform was a nightmare. Those in the audience who started out early enough probably did best of all as they were ahead of the real traffic jams. However, as early as Thursday night, when around 25,000 had made it to the festival site, there were signs of impending problems. By 11.00am on Friday the traffic on Route 17B was already backed up 10 miles to Route 17. It was like Woodstock was a magnet and nothing could resist its force in drawing people to it.

By Friday lunchtime an estimated 200,000 had poured into the festival site, creating in the process massive traffic jams. By midnight police were trying to turn people back from the regular route, trying to re-route them claiming, "Sullivan County is filled up." This meant that traffic in the Catskills was at a virtual standstill and there was a line of cars 20 miles long into the site. Police estimated that there were around 400,000 people in and around the site with still more trying to get near enough to walk the rest of the way.

One of the performers who tried to drive to Bethel was Melanie and she ended up being re-routed to a hotel where she was later picked up by helicopter; it would become a familiar pattern for many of the performers. All the performers had been booked into hotels miles from Bethel with elaborate plans to ferry them in and out by vehicles on specially organized routes. This plan didn't even get off the ground as the 'routes' had turned into parking lots. It seemed like every spare helicopter in the northeastern United States had been chartered, but their numbers were limited as this was a time when helicopters, outside of the military, were in short supply. Eventually close to twenty choppers were in service, but to begin with just small ones were available, only able to carry four people at a time.

A one point early on Friday, Rosenman and Roberts heard that New York Governor Rockefeller was thinking of declaring the festival a disaster area. At first they reasoned this might lead to some relief, but quickly someone spoke up and reminded them that it would give the Governor the right to send in the National Guard. That would not be a good idea; it was nine months before the infamous Kent State shootings but everyone was well aware of the potential for a catastrophe.

When Richie Havens finally finished his performance he flew by helicopter back to where his car was parked at one of the hotels rented by Woodstock Ventures. He then drove south to Newark Airport and he took a plane to Michigan where he was to play the next night.

"I was the only person on the New York Thruway going south."
~ Richie Havens

WOODSTOCK VOICES

"We expect a crowd of between 50,000 – 150,000."
~ Michael Lang, 27 June 1969

"Thousands Rolling in for Woodstock Rock."
~ *Washington Post* headline, Friday 15 August 1969

"Traffic uptight at Hippiefest."
~ *New York Daily News* headline, Saturday 16 August 1969

"Alex asked the pilot 'what kind of crop is that?' 'It's not a crop,' said the pilot, 'it's people.'"
~ Nancy Nevins of Sweetwater

"It's so groovy to come here and see all you people living in tents."
~ John Sebastian

"It was the only helicopter available. If it wasn't for the US Army, Woodstock might not have happened." ~ Richie Havens

"Anyone who tries to come here is crazy. Sullivan County is a great big parking lot." ~ Wes Pomeroy, Director of Security, Woodstock Music & Arts Fair, Friday 15 August 1969

"Just love everybody all around ya and clean up a little garbage on your way out and everything's gonna be alright."
~John Sebastian

"I've just been hit by lightning!"
~ Jerry Garcia

"You saw musicians getting soaked by the rain, it brought everyone down to a common reality. That was the most precious thing about the festival. The egos all melted away." ~ Jack Casady, Jefferson Airplane

"A Big Bang? I think that's a great way to describe it, because the important thing about it wasn't how many people were there or that it was a lot of truly wonderful music that got played."
~ David Crosby

"Everything was kind of disorganized in a loveable kind of way." ~ Jorma Kaukonen, Jefferson Airplane

"What brought them to Bethel is rock music – their common denominator, the distillation of the finest, the worst, the angriest, the most gentle, the happiest, the saddest thing that youth believe is in their lives." ~ *Washington Post*, Saturday 16 August 1969

"Abbie was very out of his head at Woodstock. He didn't have contact with reality." ~ Artie Kornfeld on Abbie Hoffman

"As far as I know the narcotics guys are not arresting anybody for grass. If we did there isn't enough space in Sullivan, or the next three counties to put them in."
~ A State Police sergeant

"I'll never forget the way the music sounded bouncing up against a field of bodies." ~ Carlos Santana

"If you don't have it here by tomorrow at 12 o'clock, I'm calling the Governor and having him declare this a disaster area and bring in the National Guard. I'm enraged and my colleagues here are furious at what you have not done." ~ A doctor from the Medical Committee For Human Rights

"Good morning. What we have in mind is breakfast in bed for 400,000!" ~ Wavy Gravy

"They had to sleep in the mud and rain and get hassled by this and hassled by that, and still came through saying it was a successful festival." ~ Jimi Hendrix

"One youth has died and an estimated 1,000 others have been treated . . . those hospitalized are suffering from dysentery, injuries sustained in crowds going to and leaving the concerts, and – in some cases – from reaction to drugs." ~ Radio news bulletin

"Woodstock was the last great burst of innocence in the face of the oncoming Seventies and war and hard drugs and Nixon and disco." ~ Paul Kantner, Jefferson Airplane

"Everybody was either so stoned or so tired that the performance was really bad." ~ Grace Slick, Jefferson Airplane

"We must be in heaven, man!" ~ Wavy Gravy

"I look out and see all these mouths open and asleep. But one guy way, way, way, out there flicks his lighter and he says 'Don't worry about it, John, we're with ya.' And I played the whole rest of the show to that guy." ~ John Fogerty, Creedence Clearwater Revival

"Sure. I enjoyed playing there. All my gigs are good." ~ Sly Stone

"We didn't plan it this way, but this is a free concert. There is no gate. There's no cash. It's a beautiful thing. Have some faith."
~ Michael Lang

"Two Dead as 450,000 begin Fest Exodus." ~ *The Times Herald Record,* 18 August 1969

"You aren't taking poison. The acid's not poison. It's just badly manufactured acid. You are not going to die. We have treated 300 cases and it's just all badly manufactured acid. So if you think you've taken poison, you haven't. But if you're worried, just take half a tablet." ~ Stage announcement on Saturday night

"I remember trying to fall asleep during 'The Star-Spangled Banner.' I just wished he would stop."
~ Phil Ciganer, Jerry Garcia's friend

"Don't bother Max's cows. Let them moo in peace." ~ Sign erected by someone in the audience

THE ORIGINAL RUNNING ORDER

IF ANYONE KNOWS the planned running order of the artists booked to play Woodstock they are either not telling or they have lost the piece of paper on which it was written.

The order presented here is a 'best guess' based on how much bands were paid to appear at the festival, although it's not always safe to assume that if one artist or group got more money than another, then it meant they were to be placed higher on the bill. Forceful managers, relationships between the organizers and artists, and their managers or agents, also played a part.

There was so much confusion on the first day that things got off to a bad start, nor did they recover for the duration of the weekend.

FRIDAY 15th AUGUST
Things were originally supposed to start at 4:00pm.

Sweetwater
Bert Sommer
Tim Hardin
Ravi Shankar
The Incredible String Band
Melanie
Arlo Guthrie
Richie Havens
Joan Baez

SATURDAY 16th AUGUST

Quill
Santana
The Keef Hartley Band
Mountain
Canned Heat
Grateful Dead
Janis Joplin
Sly & The Family Stone
Creedence Clearwater Revival
The Who
Jefferson Airplane

SUNDAY 17th AUGUST

Joe Cocker
Country Joe & The Fish
Sha-Na-Na
Ten Years After
Johnny Winter
The Paul Butterfield Blues Band
Crosby, Stills, Nash & Young
The Band
Blood, Sweat & Tears
Jimi Hendrix

THE BANDS

JOAN BAEZ

The Queen of Folk had been recording for a decade before appearing at Woodstock. Her relationship with Bob Dylan had been well-publicized; she brought respectability, even if she didn't sell many tickets. She had her biggest hit two years after Woodstock with one of The Band's songs.

THE BAND

The Band had been together for a decade and through their association with Bob Dylan they had a special place in many people's hearts, well before their debut album that came out in 1968.

BLOOD, SWEAT & TEARS

Blood, Sweat & Tears were a BIG band. Their second album had held the No. 1 spot on the U.S. album charts for nearly two months, only slipping in May. They had two records reach No. 2 on the singles chart, making them a big draw at Woodstock and the other festivals throughout the summer of '69.

THE PAUL BUTTERFIELD BLUES BAND

Though not a major act they were nevertheless well thought of by music fans and peers alike. Paul Butterfield always had great musicians around him; by August 1969 they were more jazzers than bluesmen, which made Woodstock not the ideal stage for their talents.

CANNED HEAT

A solid rock blues outfit who were well known for their very original singles – 'On the Road Again' and 'Going Up The Country.' They had a lot of originality, often extending the formula well beyond the standard 12-bar blues. They arguably achieved more than many would have expected when they started out; at live gigs they were always a crowd pleaser.

JOE COCKER

Prior to Woodstock his profile in America was more well-known with those in the know than most average music listeners. His cover of The Beatles' 'With A Little Help From My Friends' made No. 68 in the *Billboard* chart at the end of 1968, even though it had gone to No. 1 in Britain.

COUNTRY JOE & THE FISH

They had the perfect counter-culture pedigree having been nurtured in San Francisco's Bay Area on a heady mix of politics, music and possibly a few drugs. They were influential in formulating the sound of alternative FM radio and were stalwarts at the Fillmore West and the Avalon Ballroom when the world looked to America's West Coast for musical inspiration.

CREEDENCE CLEARWATER REVIVAL

Their consistent flow of hit records on the *Billboard* charts undermined their position as a truly creative and original rock group. Somehow they remained musical outsiders in their home city of San Francisco; they were one of the highest paid bands at Woodstock, which tells you something. They were there by right.

Creedence Clearwater Revival

CROSBY, STILLS, NASH & YOUNG

Only their second gig as a band, but they were all musical veterans even this early in their career. Between them they had probably chalked up more hit records than any act appearing at the festival. They didn't disappoint with a set full of great tunes and vocal harmonies.

THE GRATEFUL DEAD

A gargantuan name even then; the Dead were the head's band with a reputation as a crowd pleaser at festivals around the country. Playing live was what galvanized the Dead and usually produced incredible results... usually.

ARLO GUTHRIE

A singer with a pedigree that was top drawer; he had a seeming ability to do no wrong in his short career. His 'Alice's Restaurant Massacree' was a staple of alternative radio and his popularity around the campuses was up there with the best of them.

TIM HARDIN

A truly gifted songwriter whose songs were probably better known than he was. His 'How Can We Hang On To A Dream' was one of the most beautiful songs of the Sixties and could in its own way have been the theme song of the Woodstock generation.

THE KEEF HARTLEY BAND

Their appearance on the bill probably puzzled many people. Unusual in that they were a drummer led band, but his pedigree was good. Every festival needs bands that come on early and this was the lot of The Keef Hartley Band.

RICHIE HAVENS

Another veteran of the Greenwich Village folk scene; well known at festivals on both sides of the Atlantic.

He had opened for Eric Clapton's Blind Faith, which included Steve Winwood, in London's Hyde Park a month before Woodstock.

JIMI HENDRIX

Little more than two years from finding fame in Britain and a good deal less than that since he broke into the *Billboard* charts. None of his singles before Woodstock got higher than No. 20 on the American charts; ironically neither did they after the festival. Hendrix was an album seller, with *Are You Experienced, Axis: Bold As Love* and *Electric Ladyland* all making the Top 10

THE INCREDIBLE STRING BAND

Possibly the least obvious of the bigger bands booked to appear at Woodstock. Their music was much better suited to a small space, where intimacy is important. They had played both the Fillmores and were for many the embodiment of hippie idyll.

JEFFERSON AIRPLANE

For many around the world the quintessential San Francisco rock band, they were another of the Festival's big draws. With their lead singers, Grace Slick and Marty Balin, they managed to combine great music with political ideals with which most everyone in the crowd sympathized.

JANIS JOPLIN

After the demise of Big Brother & the Holding Company, Janis Joplin had carved out a solo career that musically was in a very similar groove, but it was one that was very popular across America. Her lifestyle was much the same as the one she sang about and it was beginning to take its toll.

MELANIE

A virtual unknown to almost everyone in the

Jimi Hendrix, Harlem, 9 August 1969

audience, Melanie was better known in Europe than in her homeland; Woodstock would change all that.

MOUNTAIN
Woodstock was the band's fourth gig so it's a testament to them that they pulled it off. The Cream-influenced sound was down to Felix Pappalardi who had produced the English band, but it was also because Leslie West was an exceptional guitarist.

QUILL
Almost completely unknown before opening the second day's proceedings, they would remain unknown afterwards.

SANTANA
As the band walked onstage at Woodstock their debut album was just being shipped from Columbia's warehouse to record stores across America. Little did the band or the label know just how right their timing would prove to be.

JOHN SEBASTIAN
The former leader of the Lovin' Spoonful was not even due to play so it was his good fortune that the organizers needed him to fill in a gap in the program.

SHA NA NA
Another virtual unknown whose theatrical rock'n'roll show, with a batch of tunes that practically everyone knew by heart, was the perfect set to warm up the crowd for Hendrix – Happy Days!

RAVI SHANKAR
His association with The Beatles, in particular George Harrison, gave the Indian sitar maestro impeccable credentials, even if many in the audience had never ever listened to such music before.

SLY & THE FAMILY STONE
An eclectic mix was certainly what Woodstock was all about and the inclusion of Sly Stone's rock–soul–funk was an inspired choice. He had recently topped the *Billboard* charts for four weeks with 'Everyday People.' A hit always helps.

BERT SOMMER
Another of the virtual unknowns booked to appear and despite a real talent it would be his fate to remain virtually unknown throughout his career.

SWEETWATER
A band who had released an album that had failed to garner the airplay necessary to move them up rock's rankings. They had a tricky slot and were another for whom Woodstock's magic failed.

TEN YEARS AFTER
Before Woodstock, Ten Years After were just another British rock band with a strong hint of the blues who were struggling to get closer to top billing. Things were going well for them in Britain but in America they were a virtual unknown; all that would change.

THE WHO
Despite being one of the best-paid bands at Woodstock, The Who were not that well-known in America. Their only album, prior to 1969, to achieve any success was *Magic Bus – The Who On Tour* which made No. 39 on the U.S. album chart. *Tommy* was in the process of changing all that.

JOHNNY WINTER
The Texan blues guitarist was possibly on the verge of becoming the next big thing. His debut album came out three months before the festival to less than enthusiastic reviews. Would Woodstock be the making of Johnny Winter?

Keith Moon and Pete Townshend of The Who, 1968

THE WAGES OF WOODSTOCK

AS WITH MUCH of what happened at Woodstock, precise details of who was paid what have become lost in the constant re-telling of the story. However, after much detective work, and eliminating some of the more fanciful figures that have been bandied about, it would appear that the money paid over to the performers totaled around $180,000. In 1969 the average yearly income in America was around $6,000, which puts it all into some kind of perspective.

Jimi Hendrix	$32,000
Blood, Sweat & Tears	$15,000
The Who	$12,500
Jefferson Airplane	$12,000
Creedence Clearwater revival	$11,500
Joan Baez	$10,000
Grateful Dead	$ 7,500
Sly & The Family Stone	$ 7,500
Janis Joplin	$ 7,500
The Band	$ 7,500
Canned Heat	$ 6,500
Richie Havens	$ 6,000
The Paul Butterfield Blues Band	$ 5,250
Crosby, Stills, Nash & Young	$ 5,000
Arlo Guthrie	$ 5,000
Ravi Shankar	$ 4,500
Johnny Winter	$ 3,750
Ten Years After	$ 3,250
Country Joe & The Fish	$ 2,500

The Incredible String Band	$ 2,250
Mountain	$ 2,000
Tim Hardin	$ 2,000
Santana	$ 1,500
Joe Cocker	$ 1,375
Sweetwater	$ 1,250
John Sebastian	$ 1,000
Bert Sommer	$ 1,000
Melanie	$ 750
The Keef Hartley Band	$ 500
Quill	$ 375
Sha Na Na	$ 300

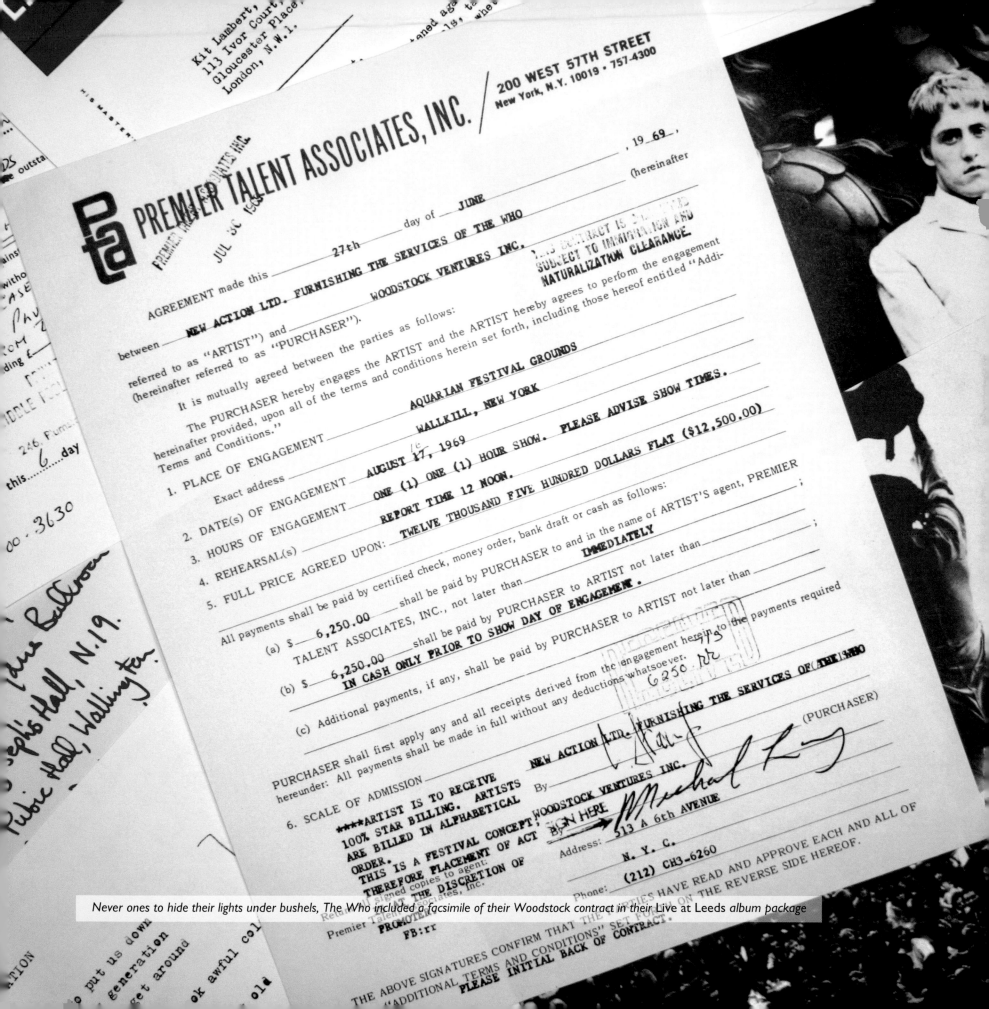

His Holiness Sri Swami Satchidananda blesses the Woodstock Festival, 15 August 1969

DAY ONE
FRIDAY 15 AUGUST 1969

Things were due to get underway at around 4:00pm but with the roads around the site, as well as in the areas leading to Bethel, clogged with cars and people, artists were finding it difficult to get to the site. Eventually Richie Havens stepped into the breach to perform a longer-than-anticipated set.

5:00pm RICHIE HAVENS

6:00pm Festival Blessing by

HIS HOLINESS SRI SWAMI SATCHIDANANDA

6:15pm SWEETWATER

7:15pm BERT SOMMER

9:00pm TIM HARDIN

10:00pm RAVI SHANKAR

11:00pm MELANIE

11:45pm ARLO GUTHRIE

1:00am JOAN BAEZ

Richie Havens kicks off the Woodstock Festival, 15 August 1969

RICHIE HAVENS

"YOU'RE THE ONLY GUY that can save us, man," is how Michael Lang got Richie Havens onstage to play what was the most important gig of his career. The twenty-eight year old Brooklyn-born singer and guitarist had already appeared in a number of festivals that summer, including opening for Blind Faith in front of 120,000 people at the free concert in London's Hyde Park in June; a month before Woodstock he appeared at the Newport Folk Festival. Havens was a veteran of the Greenwich Village folk scene along with Bob Dylan and Joan Baez, releasing his first album, *Mixed Bag*, on Verve in 1967. He had covered many Lennon and McCartney songs on his four albums that came out before the Woodstock Festival and their songs featured heavily during his set. It seems likely that he performed some other Beatles' tunes during his performance, but the precise details have been lost to the mists of time.

PERFORMANCE
Originally Richie Havens was slated to play maybe four songs, but with bands stuck in traffic, logistical issues with the equipment and the all-pervasive mayhem he just kept on playing. Havens himself has said in the past that he played for over two hours, but this is an exaggeration as other acts that followed him played in the daylight, so about an hour is probably closer to the truth. However there is no question that his repertoire was stretched to the limit as 'Freedom,' his encore, was pretty much made up as he went along.

"We've finally made it! We did it this time – they'll never be able to hide us again!" ~ Richie Havens greeting the Woodstock crowd

THE WOODSTOCK EFFECT
Richie Havens ever after called his Woodstock appearance, "career making." And what a long career it's been. Almost thirty albums over the last five decades have produced few hit singles – his only success on the singles chart in America was The Beatles' 'Here Comes The Sun' in 1971, and there have been none in Britain. Similarly he's only had one significant U.S. album, *Alarm Clock*, in 1971, yet he's an instantly recognizable performer, in part because of his appearance in the *Woodstock* film. A committed man, who has never stopped campaigning for a better world, he is living proof that hits don't matter, it's the taking part that counts.

Alarm Clock   (1971)

60-MINUTE SET

SET LIST

High Flyin' Bird
Minstrel From Gault
I Can't Make It Anymore
Handsome Johnny
With A Little Help From My Friends
Strawberry Fields Forever/Hey Jude
Hey Jude
Freedom
Possibly others

THE BAND
Richie Havens - Guitar, Vocals
Daniel Ben Zebulon - Percussion, Conga
Paul "Deano" Williams – Guitar

**FRIDAY
15 AUGUST**

SWEETWATER

AS THE FIRST BAND to appear on stage at Woodstock it's perhaps surprising that Sweetwater are not better known. The band originated in Los Angeles, getting together in 1968 when singer Nancy Nevins walked into a bar where some of the other members were playing. She sang the old blues tune 'Motherless Child' and ended up joining the band. Their sound and ethos were very 'West Coast' featuring an unusual line-up of instruments, most notably with no lead guitar and an experimental sound that some have compared to Jefferson Airplane, most likely because both bands, unusually, featured a female lead vocalist. There's also more than a hint of Spanky and Our Gang and The Mamas & The Papas in their harmonious vocal arrangements.

Sweetwater (1968)

The band signed to Reprise Records and released their album *Sweetwater*, in 1968. It was a somewhat unfocused affair with its jazz overtones, along with straight-ahead rock and even some classical inflections. However, that's with the benefit of hindsight, at the time there were many bands whose debut albums were perhaps not the 'fully formed sound' for which they might later become famous. Sweetwater was produced by Dave Hassinger who had also worked with The Rolling Stones, so it certainly sounded very good.

"We were definitely the sound check!" ~ Nancy Nevins

PERFORMANCE
The majority of Sweetwater's set was taken from their debut album. 'Look Out' and 'Day Song' both come from *Just For You*, their second album, which was not released until after Nancy Nevin's accident. Both these songs were composed by Nancy and recorded by the band before she was so sadly injured.

THE WOODSTOCK EFFECT
In December 1969, with work on their second album under way, Nancy Nevins was hit by a truck; it put the twenty-year-old singer into a coma from which it took months to recover. While the band soldiered on, finishing off the album with other members taking on the vocal duties, Nancy was unable to rejoin to help them capitalize on any potential success. In fact she spent a long time in therapy and, while the band did make a third album, they broke up in 1971. They did reform in 1999 with three original members, including Nancy Nevins, and VH1 made a TV movie called *Sweetwater: A True Rock Story*.

45-MINUTE SET

SET LIST
Motherless Child
Look Out
For Pete's Sake
Day Song
What's Wrong
My Crystal Spider
Two Worlds
Why Oh Why

THE BAND
Nancy Nevins - Vocals
Alex Del Zoppo - Keyboards
Fred Herrera - Bass
August Burns - Cello
Alan Malarowitz - Drums
Elpidio 'Pete' Cobian - Conga, Drums
Albert Moore - Flute, Backing Vocals

FRIDAY 15 AUGUST

BERT SOMMER

The Road To Travel (1969)

BERT SOMMER'S first album *The Road To Travel* came out in 1968; it was made under the direction of Capitol's A&R man Artie Kornfield so it's none too difficult to work out why he played Woodstock. However, it would be too easy to say it was just a case of record company nepotism. Sommer was much more talented than that.

The first time the world heard Bert sing was on a single by Bert and Bill in 1967; later that year he joined the Left Banke, although it was after they had their hits. His next break came when he got the part of Woof in the original Broadway production of *Hair*. This was when Bert met Artie Kornfield and they began working together. His voice was a wonderful instrument so why isn't he better known? Of course there's luck and the fact that he didn't appear on the original *Woodstock* movie, although he can be seen in *Woodstock Diaries* performing 'Jennifer.'

PERFORMANCE

Twenty-year-old Sommer went on stage and opened with 'Jennifer': it's about singer Jennifer Warnes with whom he appeared in *Hair*. "Smile and the world smiles with you," as Bert Sommer sings in his song, appropriately named

Inside Bert Sommer (1970)

> **"Bert Sommer should have been someone accepted on the same level as any of the superstars that played at Woodstock."**
> ~ Artie Kornfield

'Smile,' may not be the most original line but his material on the strength of these two songs made for a perfect set on Folk-Friday. Most of what he sang came from his first album, although 'America' and 'Smile' come from his second album *Inside Bert Sommer*, released on the Eleuthera label, recorded around the time of his Woodstock appearance.

THE WOODSTOCK EFFECT

Ironically he had one very small hit, 'We're All Playing in the Same Band,' from his second album that crept into the Top 50 almost a year to the day after he played at Woodstock. After his first two albums he released a self-titled album in 1970 on Buddah. It would be another seven years before his next, another self-titled album on Capitol. In the 80s Sommer, anxious to get back into the business of making records, cut a demo called 'Heart of the City.' It's one of those great undiscovered gems. Bert Sommer passed away in July 1990, a great lost talent who nearly was, who left his music to tell his story.

45-MINUTE SET

SET LIST
'Jennifer'
'The Road to Travel'
'I Wondered Where You Be'
'She's Gone'
'Things Are Goin' My Way'
'And When It's Over'
'Jeanette'
'America'
'A Note That Read'
'Smile'

THE BAND
Bert Sommer - Guitar, Vocals
Charlie Bilello - Bass
Ira Stone - Guitar, Organ, Harmonica

FRIDAY 15 AUGUST

Tim Hardin backstage at Woodstock, August 1969.

TIM HARDIN

ANYONE WITH AN INTEREST IN THE MUSIC of the last fifty years will know Tim Hardin's songs. 'If I Were a Carpenter,' 'Misty Roses,' 'Reason to Believe' and 'Lady Came From Baltimore' have been covered by hundreds of artists, ranging from The Carpenters to Bobby Darin, Rod Stewart to Scott Walker. The folk singer and songwriter born in Eugene, Oregon in December 1941 was hardly a household name when Hardin walked on stage at Woodstock. Ironically his recording of 'Simple Song of Freedom' was at No. 61 on the *Billboard* chart, his one and only hit record in America; it was written, not by this gifted songwriter, but by Bobby Darin.

Hardin, discharged from the Marines in 1961, was appearing regularly in Greenwich Village by 1964. He signed to Verve in 1966 releasing the first of four albums with the label; on that first record was the beautiful 'How Can We Hang On To a Dream.' Hardin's second album included 'If I Were a Carpenter,' which Bobby Darin took into the Top 10 in 1966, around the time that Hardin moved to Woodstock. By the time of his appearance at the festival Hardin was with Columbia Records working on the album that became *Suite For Susan Moore and Damion.*

Tim Hardin I (1966)

Tim Hardin 2 (1967)

PERFORMANCE

Hardin had been expected to perform earlier but his drug problems made that impossible. It also made it difficult for his backing musicians to perform with him. The only record of Tim's performance is the recording of 'If I Were a Carpenter,' which he sang alone.

> ## "After a while we played and, I must say, not well. To everyone's disappointment, Tim Hardin was more stoned that we would have wanted."
>
> ~ Steve 'Muruga' Booker

THE WOODSTOCK EFFECT

Susan Moore (Morss) was Hardin's wife and shortly after his appearance at Woodstock she left him, taking their son Damion with her. Hardin moved to Britain, registering as a heroin addict to obtain drugs from the National Health Service. He made several albums in the Seventies; they all failed to live up to their predecessors. He returned to America in the mid-Seventies, but sadly died a week after his 39th birthday, failing to get recognition during his lifetime and after. Richard Bock later became principal cellist with the Phoenix Symphony Orchestra, while Ralph Towner and Glen Moore are much-respected jazz players.

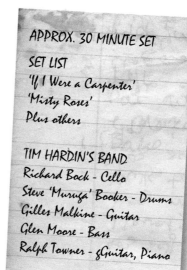

APPROX. 30 MINUTE SET

SET LIST
'If I Were a Carpenter'
'Misty Roses'
Plus others

TIM HARDIN'S BAND
Richard Bock - Cello
Steve 'Muruga' Booker - Drums
Gilles Malkine - Guitar
Glen Moore - Bass
Ralph Towner - gGuitar, Piano

**FRIDAY
15 AUGUST**

Ravi Shankar performing at the Monterey Festival, Sunday 18 June 1967

RAVI SHANKAR

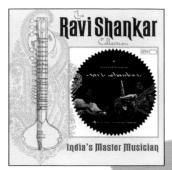

India's Master Musician
(1963)

RAVI SHANKAR CAME to fame in the west through his association with George Harrison, who took up the sitar and first played it on 'Norwegian Wood' on The Beatles' *Rubber Soul* album in 1965; George had been introduced to the sitar by David Crosby who back then was with The Byrds.

Subsequent Beatles albums all had something of an Indian aspect about them. The Bengali sitar player was born in 1920 and started playing on stage aged just 10. Having finished his formal training in 1944 he began recording for an Indian record label as well as composing music for films and ballet (he later wrote music for the 1982 film *Gandhi*), Shankar's association with The Beatles made him the premier Indian musician in the eyes of western musicians and his first festival appearance was at the Monterey Festival in 1967. His fame and acceptance by western fans excited him and he enjoyed seeing his music embraced by them, but sometimes it frustrated him that Indian culture seemed to be treated as some kind of cultural takeaway. "They all became part of a cocktail that everyone seemed to be lapping up." The 'they' included yoga, the *Kama Sutra* and hashish.

PERFORMANCE
The first and the last pieces feature all three players while 'Jhaptal' is a tabla solo. Appropriately both the pieces played by Ravi Shankar are evening ragas. The last, and longer raga highlights some amazing interplay between Shankar and Rakha, the tabla player.

> **"I was knocked out by him! Just as a person, He's an incredible fellow. He's one of the greatest."**
> ~ George Harrison

THE WOODSTOCK EFFECT
Ravi Shankar joined his friend George Harrison at the Concert for Bangladesh at Madison Square Garden in August 1971 and was heavily featured on the subsequent album, which further enhanced his standing with western fans. In 2001 Shankar's daughter, Anoushka, and a group of Indian musicians played a piece composed by Ravi and appeared with other musicians, including Paul McCartney and Eric Clapton, at the Concert for George following the Beatle's passing. Shankar's other daughter is the jazz singer Norah Jones, whose Grammy-winning album *Come Away With Me* has sold over 20 million copies around the world. The respect with which his peers hold Shankar is reflected by the fact that those he has collaborated with include Yehudi Menuhin and Philip Glass.

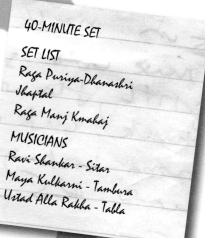

40-MINUTE SET

SET LIST
Raga Puriya-Dhanashri
Jhaptal
Raga Manj Kmahaj

MUSICIANS
Ravi Shankar - Sitar
Maya Kulkarni - Tambura
Ustad Alla Rakha - Tabla

**FRIDAY
15 AUGUST**

MELANIE

A NATIVE NEW YORKER, Melanie Safka got to play at Woodstock because her management company had an office in the same building as the Woodstock Ventures office; the 22-year-old just asked them if she could play and they were more than happy for her to appear. She is unique among the artists in that she was directly inspired to write a hit song following her appearance.

Clive Davis signed Melanie to Columbia with a view to making her into a pop artist, but according to the singer herself, "I was still considered a little too weird to be mainstream, so they allowed Buddah to buy out my contract." Melanie recorded an album, which did nothing in America but gave her a No. 1 in France with 'Bobo's Party.' She also had a hit in Holland with 'Beautiful People,' one of the two songs she sang at Woodstock.

"I drove up there, just me, my guitar and my mother." ~ Melanie

PERFORMANCE
When Melanie went on stage she was confronted with the sea of people, many of whom had lit candles, which became the inspiration for her song 'Lay Down (Candles in the Rain).' All she sang were the two songs, in something of a wavering voice because she was so nervous.

THE WOODSTOCK EFFECT
She recorded 'Lay Down (Candles in the Rain)' with the Edwin Hawkins Singers which completely

Gather Me (1972)

captured the Woodstock moment, bringing her huge success the world over. She followed this with 'Peace Will Come' which was a minor hit, before releasing her cover of The Rolling Stones' 'Ruby Tuesday' which did only moderately in the U.S.A. but went Top 10 in Britain and many other European countries. In 1971 she issued her biggest single 'Brand New Key' which topped the American charts and was another Top 10 record around the world. None of Melanie's three albums from which these singles were taken did particularly well in America with the best of them, *Gather Me*, only reaching No. 15 in early 1972. This album and 'Brand New Key' were on the Neighborhood label, which Melanie founded with her husband.

From this point on Melanie withdrew from recording and appearing to raise her daughter but came back in 1976 to make an album with Ahmet Ertegun. Although much of her work since then has been warmly received she has not had the commercial success that others with less talent have achieved. Recently she has received some well-deserved attention from other musicians and the public who have finally recognized that she is worthy of being placed alongside other great women singers.

15-MINUTE SET

SET LIST
Beautiful People
Birthday Of The Sun

THE BAND
Just Melanie and her guitar

**FRIDAY
15 AUGUST**

73

ARLO GUTHRIE

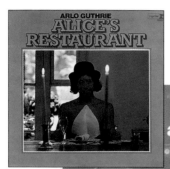

Alice's Restaurant (1967)

ARLO GUTHRIE'S pedigree is top drawer. He's the son of legendary folk singer Woody Guthrie (he died in 1967 after a long battle with Huntington's disease) and he was born on Coney Island, New York in 1947. Growing up around other legendary singers, friends of his father's that included Leadbelly and Pete Seeger, led to Arlo giving his first public performance in 1960. He had 'second homes' at New York's Gaslight and Bitter End clubs and by 1967 he had his first record deal with Reprise Records releasing the album *Alice's Restaurant*. The centrepiece of his debut was 'Alice's Restaurant Massacree,' an 18-minute anti-Vietnam-War satirical protest song that is based on Arlo's own true-life rejection for military service on account of him having a criminal record.

'Alice's Restaurant Massacree' was a mainstay of campus radio stations and established his credentials as a spokesman for many who shared his anti-war stance and hippie ideals; the album made No. 17 on the U.S. album chart in early 1968. His follow-up, *Arlo*, did not capture the public's imagination in the same way, but in 1969 his album *Running Down the Road* included 'Coming into Los Angeles' which on its release as a single almost got him into the charts.

40-MINUTE SET

SET LIST
Coming into Los Angeles
Walking Down the Line
Amazing Grace

ARLO'S BAND
Arlo Guthrie - Guitar, Vocals
Bob Arkin - Bass
Paul Motian - Drums
John Pilla - Guitar

**FRIDAY
15 AUGUST**

"I remember standing backstage and somebody yelling 'Arlo you have to get up there and play because Richie has been up there for days.'" ~ Arlo Guthrie

PERFORMANCE
In front of the growing crowd eager to hear some songs they knew and loved, Arlo's performance left something to be desired. Whatever fun he had been having backstage definitely had a negative effect on his performance. 'Coming into Los Angeles,' his homage to beating the customs men at LA Airport went down well, but from there it seems like things went slightly down hill as he interrupted Bob Dylan's 'Walking Down the Line' with some hippie philosophizing.

THE WOODSTOCK EFFECT
Arlo's appearance at Woodstock came just a few days before the premiere of the feature film *Alice's Restaurant*, based on his song, in which he starred. This propelled Guthrie briefly into a more mainstream audience – there was even a cut-down version of the song that scraped into the *Billboard* charts. Over the next four decades Guthrie released more than 25 albums and while he has rarely had great success on the charts he remains a much-loved concert performer around the world.

Arlo Guthrie at Woodstock, 15 August 1969

JOAN BAEZ

WHEN JOAN BAEZ PERFORMED at Woodstock she could rightly be called the Queen of Folk Music, it was a fact that clearly justified her fee of $10,000, making her the second-highest-paid individual artist; she was also pregnant.

She was born to an Anglo-Scottish mother and Mexican father on 9 January 1941 on Staten Island, New York. Albert Baez, Joan's father, was a physicist who not only wrote a widely used textbook for schools, but it was his apparent refusal to work on the building of the U.S. atomic bomb which had a profound effect on Joan and was a catalyst for her activism which has lasted throughout her entire career. Joan and her family moved to Boston where her father taught at M.I.T.; Albert would take Joan and her sisters to Tulla's Coffee Grinder in the city; here they encouraged floor singers and she was soon singing there regularly. After a spell at university in Boston, studying theater, she became a regular at other local clubs that included Club 47 in Cambridge Massachusetts; she was further inspired having seen Pete Seeger in concert in 1957.

Her first recording was in 1958 in the basement of a friend's house and the following year Bob Gibson, the folk singer, invited her to perform two duets with him at Newport in front of 13,000 people. Refusing an offer from the giant Columbia Records, Baez signed to the much smaller Vanguard label and released her first album in 1960. In April 1961 she met

Joan Baez (1960)

SATURDAY
16 AUGUST

"The world I was heading into…. was really the world of Jack Elliott and Joan Baez." ~ Bob Dylan recalling heading to New York in 1961 in *Chronicles, Volume 1*

Bob Dylan in Greenwich Village and championed him and his music. Dylan was very much her protégé and joined her on stage two years later at both the Monterey and the Newport Folk festivals, the two singers became lovers.

In August 1963, she performed Pete Seeger's 'We Shall Overcome' at Miles College in Birmingham, Alabama; this live recording was released and made No. 90 in the U.S. singles chart at the end of the same year. It was the first time that people, outside of the folk scene, had heard anything very much of Baez, but this protest song was to become synonymous with her name, a beacon for her political beliefs, beliefs from which she has never shirked. She participated in peace and civil rights rallies whenever she felt the call. During 1964 she refused to pay 60% of her taxes because of government armaments expenditure. In the following May she participated in a protest march in London with the singer Donovan against the U.S. involvement in the Vietnam war; they topped it off by performing in Trafalgar Square. During her stay in Britain she appeared at the Royal Albert Hall as 'We Shall Overcome' reached No. 26 on the UK chart in the summer 1965. Later in the year 'There But For Fortune' got to No. 8 in the U.K. but

Joan Baez on stage at Woodstock, 16 August 1969.

Eric Von Schmidt's poster for the 1965 tour of Joan Baez and Bob Dylan

single did anything on the U.S. charts. In the summer of 1966 she had another British hit with 'Pack Up Your Sorrows' (No. 50). It was a song written by Richard Farina (the husband of Joan's sister Mimi), who had been killed in a motorcycle accident two years before. In the same year, she took part in a peace festival and an anti-draft demonstration, resulting in a ten-day jail sentence; this only served to harden her attitude and intensified her opposition to the war in Vietnam. Baez also married; perhaps inevitably it was another who had a history of protest, draft-resister David Harris, for whom she made *David's Album* in 1968 in Nashville. Harris was in prison while Baez played at Woodstock. His refusal to accept the draft caused the government to finally react and he was given a three-year sentence.

"The easiest kind of relationship is with ten thousand people, the hardest is with one." ~ Joan Baez

PERFORMANCE

Jeffrey Shurtleff and Richard Festinger were members of the Draft Resistance organization, which had been founded by David Harris. Apart from the traditional songs, some long associated with Joan, she played The Byrds' song 'Drug Store Truck Driving Man,' composed by Roger McGuinn and Gram Parsons. Before they performed this song about a KKK killing, Shurtleff dedicated it to the Governor of California and future president Ronald Reagan.

David's Album (1968)

could only make No. 50 in America.

In early 1965, Baez and Dylan's relationship ended but it didn't stop her recording his material and she had hits in Britain with 'It's All Over Now Baby Blue' (No. 22) and 'Farewell Angelina' (No. 35); neither

Diamonds & Rust (1975)

When Baez walked on stage at Woodstock she was the perfect artist to close what was a chaotic day. Her experience and her beautiful voice seemed to bring about a feeling of calm. She was pregnant with her son Gabriel Harris who was born in December 1969. Rain began falling heavily shortly after Joan left the stage at around 1.45am.

THE WOODSTOCK EFFECT

The year after appearing at Woodstock Joan appeared at the Isle of Wight Festival. In the summer of 1971 Baez had her biggest American hit when her version of The Band's 'The Night They Drove Old Dixie Down' got to No. 3 in America; it also became a big hit in Britain making No. 6. It was the last time that she made the Top 10 on either side of the Atlantic, to be fair Joan Baez was hardly a singles artist; albums were her forte.

For the increasingly respected singer the 1970s were all about making albums and in 1975 she had a hit with 'Diamonds & Rust', taken from the album of the same name; it was an autobiographical song about her romantic involvement with Dylan. Throughout the next three decades Joan Baez has remained a tireless peace and civil rights campaigner; successfully lobbying President Carter over the Vietnamese boat people and opposing the right-wing coup in Chile. She starred opposite Dylan in the film *Renaldo and Clara*, performed at the Philadelphia Live Aid concert, took part in the seventh annual Prince's Trust rock gala at the NEC Birmingham in 1989, been honoured by universities with degrees and throughout the 21st Century she has never been far from a cause, as well as appearing frequently on stage both as a solo artist and as collaborator.

45-MINUTE SET

SET LIST
'Oh Happy Day'
'The Last Thing On My Mind'
'I Shall Be Released'

Story about how the Federal Marshalls came to take David Harris into custody

'Joe Hill'
'Sweet Sir Galahad'
'Hickory Wind'
'Drug Store Truck Driving Man'
'I Live One Day At A Time'
'Sweet Sunny South'
'Warm and Tender Love'

'Swing Low Sweet Chariot'
'We Shall Overcome'

ACCOMPANYING JOAN BAEZ
Richard Festinger - Guitar
Jeffrey Shurtleff - Vocals, Guitar

DAY TWO
SATURDAY 16 AUGUST 1969

The day got underway well enough, but the production staff were soon battling against time as the bands were not always ready to go on, which is why both Country Joe and John Sebastian were introduced into the line-up. This entertained the crowd, but pushed timings further backwards. The Dead's heavy equipment partially broke the turntable designed to speed up change-overs; from that point on everything went slower.

12:15pm QUILL
1:00pm COUNTRY JOE MCDONALD
2:00pm SANTANA
3:30pm JOHN SEBASTIAN
4:45pm THE KEEF HARTLEY BAND
6:00pm THE INCREDIBLE STRING BAND
7:30pm CANNED HEAT
9:00pm MOUNTAIN
10:30pm GRATEFUL DEAD
12:30am CREEDENCE CLEARWATER REVIVAL
2:00am JANIS JOPLIN
3:30am SLY & THE FAMILY STONE
5:00am THE WHO
7:30am JEFFERSON AIRPLANE

QUILL

FORMED BY THE BROTHERS Dan and Joe Cole, the appearance of Quill at Woodstock was supposed to be their finest hour, if only anyone could really remember anything much about it. Having plugged away on the North East tour circuit for over two years the band had made little headway. It was after an appearance at Steve Paul's Scene in New York City that they got their chance to appear at the festival. During the build-up to the festival itself they apparently played at various other venues around the Woodstock area. These included the motel housing most of the crew building the stage and organizing the site, along with a state prison and a mental institution; it seems it was neither their Folsom Prison, nor a cuckoo's nest. Among these pre-festival events was a show for Bethel residents who sat on the grass and probably didn't know quite what to make of it.

Shortly before Woodstock Quill were signed to Cotillion, a subsidiary of Atlantic Records, but their album was not available before the festival meaning they had no profile at all, ensuring them the place as the opening act. Sadly, problems with the sound system and technical problems with the filming of their performance meant they missed out on even one

> 30-MINUTE SET
>
> THE SET LIST
> 'That's How I Eat'
> 'Driftin''
> 'They Live the Life'
> 'Waitin' for You'
>
> THE BAND
> Jon Cole - Bass, Vocals
> Dan Cole - Vocals
> Roger North - Drums
> Norman Rogers - Guitar, Vocals
> Phil Thayer - Keyboard,
> Saxophone, Flute

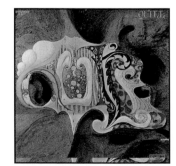

Quill (1969)

"A self-indulgent mess with some promise and much racket." ~ A review of Quill's first and only album

minute of fame. Some footage that does survive seems to have been over-dubbed, as the percussion sounds are far too clear given a lack of any amplification.

PERFORMANCE

When Quill played on the club circuit they had a neat little trick of handing out percussion instruments to the crowd and getting them to join in. For several hundred people in a club it worked very well and it's been claimed they could drive the audience to "a near riotous dance frenzy." When they tried this at Woodstock the logistics of getting hundreds of thousands to participate proved overwhelming and the audience were underwhelmed.

THE WOODSTOCK EFFECT

The *Quill* album was self-produced and it failed to either capitalize on whatever reputation had been garnered from their Woodstock appearance or even give one member of the band much hope of success. Jon Cole the bass-playing vocalist, left the band to pursue his own musical interests and Cotillion lost whatever enthusiasm they had for promoting the band, and they died a musical death; despite recording a follow-up album as a four-piece that the label didn't even bother releasing. Only Roger North seems to have continued with a musical career: he played with the Holy Modal Rounders but never had any significant success.

COUNTRY JOE McDONALD

COUNTRY JOE'S BACKGROUND was Scottish Presbyterian, which may explain why he became so involved in left-wing political activism; on the other hand it may not. Joseph Allen McDonald took his name from 'Country Joe' Stalin which had been a popular nickname for the wartime Russian leader during the 1940s. He sang around the Bay Area folk clubs and later co-edited the folk music magazine *Rag Baby*.

The first record he made as Country Joe and The Fish was 'I-Feel-Like-I'm-Fixin'-To-Die Rag' back in 1966; originally it was recorded very much in the jug band style. After the magazine folded, Rag Baby operated as a record company releasing an EP by Country Joe and the Fish. The band signed to Elektra and from then on it was electric music for the mind and body.

"We all used to be folkies, but we changed to rock because we found folk wasn't our music. The words and music should be a total experience, and it should be a hippy experience." ~ Country Joe McDonald, December 1966

PERFORMANCE
Country Joe came on to 'fill up a gap in the program,' helping the organizers cope with the turn-rounds between groups. His relaxed sing-along style was perfect for the sunny afternoon; Joe had been a busker in Berkeley, California in the early 1960s, although it was a slightly larger crowd than he'd been used to on Telegraph Avenue. 'Janis' came from Country Joe & the Fish's debut album; The 'Fish Cheer' and 'I-Feel-Like-I'm-Fixin'-To-Die Rag' from the band's second album while 'Rocking All Over the World' didn't get recorded until 1970, appearing on *C.J. Fish*.

Originally when the band performed the F-I-S-H Cheer the audience spelled it correctly, but in the summer of 1968 it somehow got changed to F-*-C-K and Country Joe was still doing it that way at Woodstock.

"Listen people, I don't know how you expect to ever stop the war if you can't sing any better than that, there's about 300,000 of you f*ckers out there, I want you to start singing!" ~ Country Joe McDonald during the F-I-S-H Cheer

30-MINUTE SET

SET LIST
Janis
Rockin' All Over The World
Flyin' High
I Seen a Rocket
F-I-S-H Cheer/I-Feel-Like-I'm-Fixin'-To-Die Rag

THE BAND
Just Country Joe, his guitar and headband

SATURDAY 16 AUGUST

SANTANA

A MAN, A BAND, OR A STYLE OF MUSIC? For many of us it's all three, but the genesis of Santana were very different from what many people might imagine. The band was originally called the Santana Blues Band, but not because Carlos Santana was the leader; it was just that his name flowed more freely with 'blues band' than any one of the other original members. Santana, the man, had moved to San Francisco from Tijuana, where his father was a mariachi musician whose band the teenage Carlos played in for a while. The twenty-year-old Mexican got his first break at a Sunday matinee show at the Fillmore Auditorium in San Francisco when Mike Bloomfield allowed him to sit in with his band.

> **"'Hey, I've got a friend from Tijuana who plays the blues. Can he come up and jam?' Michael was really kind, and said "Sure, come on up."** ~ Carlos Santana

In the audience at the Fillmore was a young, white keyboard player from suburban San Francisco named Gregg Rolie; he found out where Carlos was scraping a living by washing dishes and went round to ask him to come play some music with him. To earn a few dollars, Rolie was in William Penn & His Pals whose onstage attire consisted of ruffled shirts; unsurprisingly his aspirations lay elsewhere. Soon the Santana Blues Band was formed around Carlos and Rolie and to begin with they played small gigs and concerts in San Francisco's local parks. Initially the multi-racial group, which was modeled on Sly Stone's band, had a black bassist, Dave Brown; a Latino conga-player, Mike Carabello, and a white drummer, Doc Livingston. Bill Graham took an interest in the band and gave them support slots with The Who and The Butterfield Blues Band, but as they were about to play a prestigious slot on a Steve Miller/Howlin' Wolf bill, Carlos was confirmed as having tuberculosis and spent six months in hospital.

After coming out of hospital Carlos appeared for the first time on record, not with the rest of the band but as a guest on one song at a concert recorded at the Fillmore with Al Kooper and Mike Bloomfield on 26-28 September 1968. Having recorded the first two days Bloomfield, whose drug use was rampant, failed to show up for the third day, which is how Carlos came to be asked to appear; he did it as a favour for Bill Graham who had done so much to support the band.

Shortly after the Fillmore gig Santana, the band, was signed by Clive Davis to Columbia; by this time they had dropped the 'blues band' tag and changed their line-up. Despite their name the band was not run by Carlos, it was very much a democratic unit – one man, one vote. Marcus Malone had replaced Carabello and in January they began work on their album in Los Angeles but just as they did Malone was arrested for killing a man – he was apparently having an affair with his wife. Back came Carabello and with him the diminutive Nicaraguan timbales player, Jose 'Chepito' Areas. Drummer Livingston also went, mainly because of his drinking, and in came Michael Shrieve, a brilliant young musician

SATURDAY 16 AUGUST

93

Santana (1969)

who had appeared at the very same Kooper and Bloomfield jam show as Carlos a few months earlier.

This line-up recorded their debut album and in so doing created the sound on which their reputation was established, one that has stood the test of time and lasted for five decades. To Carlos Santana's blues leanings were added Jose 'Chepito' Areas' love of Latin music, and of Tito Puente in particular. Carabello favoured the 'psychedelic soul' sounds of Sly & the Family Stone and Jimi Hendrix, while Gregg Rolie was very much influenced by the sound of the 'British Invasion' and what trailed in its wake.

They had recorded their first album in May '69, and when the band went onstage at Woodstock it was just being shipped from Columbia's warehouse to record stores across America. Little did the band or the label know just how right was their timing.

PERFORMANCE

Bill Graham was the band's manager and it was he who took Santana to Woodstock.

Arguably it was one of the best musical moves he ever made as the band benefited as much, if not more, than any other performer who appeared at the festival and in their case in the movie as well.

The band's set was virtually a run through of their debut album, with just 'Fried Neckbones' as the only

CBS RECORDS IN ASSOCIATION WITH ROBERT PATERSON PRESENT TWO GREAT CONTEMPORARY CONCERTS

ROYAL ALBERT HALL
(General Manager F J Mundy)
Tickets available from 21st March
Prices 35s, 30s, 25s, 20s, 15s, 8s
Available from the Booking Office
Royal Albert Hall
and from usual agents
No telephone bookings

Friday April 17th 7.30pm
Compère John Peel
FLOCK
STEAMHAMMER
JOHNNY WINTER

Saturday April 18th 7.30pm
Compère John Peel
TAJ MAHAL
IT'S A BEAUTIFUL DAY
SANTANA

SOUNDS OF THE 70's FLY PAN-AM

song not to feature on *Santana*. Nothing could have prepared the crowd for Santana's set which was perfect 'get up and dance' music to put the crowd in the mood.

"It was scary – the dynamism that emanated from the band, and from the people themselves. Bill Graham really busted his chops to put us there." ~ Carlos Santana on the band's Woodstock appearance

45-MINUTE SET

SET LIST
Waiting
You Just Don't Care
Savor
Jingo
Persuasion
Soul Sacrifice
Fried Neckbones

THE BAND
Carlos Santana - Guitar
Gregg Rolie - Vocals, Keyboards
Jose "Chepito" Areas - Percussion
Mike Carabello - Congas
Michael Shrieve - Drums
David Brown - Bass

Abraxas (1970)

THE WOODSTOCK EFFECT

Santana, the band, the man and the sound have had a career since Woodstock that the man himself could scarcely have dreamed of when he walked on stage at around 2.00pm on Saturday afternoon. Two months after Woodstock they had their first hit record when 'Jingo' entered the *Billboard* chart, by December it had climbed to No. 56 in the charts before falling away. 'Jingo' was the first of over 25 hit singles that Carlos Santana has had during a career which has seen his band go through countless different incarnations. It wasn't until 1999 that Carlos Santana had his first No. 1 single in America with 'Smooth' and then a year later he had another with 'Maria Maria.' There have also been well over twenty Santana albums as well as collaborations with others, including John McLaughlin and jazz man Wayne Shorter.

The Very Best of Santana (1996)

> "When I hit that note – if I hit it correctly – I'm just as important as Jimi Hendrix, Eric Clapton or anybody. Because when I hit that note, I hit the umbilical cord of anybody who is listening."
>
> ~ Carlos Santana

JOHN SEBASTIAN

ANOTHER NATIVE NEW YORKER, John Sebastian was the son of a virtuoso harmonica player and he only got to play Woodstock by accident. His first group was the Even Dozen Jug Band, followed by The Mugwumps, before he found great success with The Lovin' Spoonful. Formed in 1965, the band was named after a Mississippi John Hurt blues song and they enjoyed great success on the charts. Their first hit in late summer of '65 was the wonderful 'Do You Believe in Magic,' a song written by Sebastian. There followed a string of hit singles, mostly written by Sebastian, either alone or with other members of the band, including the seminal summer song 'Summer in the City' in 1966. Few people managed to capture the spirit of mid-Sixties America better than The Lovin' Spoonful and no other songwriter articulated it as well.

In 1967, the band fell apart after Zal Yanosky and Steve Boone were busted for possession of marijuana and less than a year later Sebastian left to pursue the inevitable solo career. He had his first hit in early 1969 with the beautiful 'She's A Lady' and looked set to carry on with many more hits, helped by his appearance in the *Woodstock* movie.

30-MINUTE SET

SET LIST
How Have You Been?
Rainbows All Over Your Blues
I Had a Dream
Darlin' Be Home Soon
Younger Generation

John Sebastian – Guitar
Accompanied throughout on his
tie-dye!

PERFORMANCE
Many Lovin' Spoonful songs could just as easily have been Sebastian solo records and so it's no surprise that his Woodstock set mixed new and old material. John went on stage as a favor, having cadged a ride to the festival on board the helicopter carrying The Incredible String Band. He had not intended to perform and borrowed Tim Hardin's guitar in order to entertain the crowd while the stage was being dried

**SATURDAY
16 AUGUST**

"It's disappointing that future generations have that as my most highly visible performance."
~ John Sebastian

following the rain. He had popped some pills before going on, having no idea he would be asked to perform. Despite it all, his performance is charming and while he was clearly stoned, his particular brand of hippie psychology jived with everyone.

THE WOODSTOCK EFFECT
In 1970 he released the album *John B. Sebastian*, which included 'She's a Lady,' 'How Have You Been?,' 'Rainbows All Over Your Blues' and 'I Had a Dream'.

John B. Sebastian   (1970)

It was a wonderful album that should have done better than No. 20 on the album charts, but it was hampered by a legal dispute between Kama Sutra, Sebastian's old label, and his new one, Reprise. Two more albums followed but did not do very well at all. With his solo career stalling he composed the theme to the TV series *Welcome Back Kotter*. 'Welcome Back' went to No. 1 on the *Billboard* chart in 1976. Subsequently Sebastian has not had any significant commercial success; he's worked with mandolin player David Grisman and still tours with his own jug band. He should be revered as one of America's greatest writers of pop songs.

John Sebastian backstage at Woodstock, August 1969

THE KEEF HARTLEY BAND

ANOTHER BAND WHOSE APPEARANCE at Woodstock was more happenstance than through their achievements as a band of international stature. The Buddy Rich-inspired Keith Hartley, who had been Ringo Starr's replacement in the Liverpool band, Rory Storm and The Hurricanes, formed the band in 1968. The Keef (Cockney-speak for Keith) Hartley Band were a blues-based band who were yet another act to have suffered from failing to be included in the *Woodstock* movie or the albums.

Art Gallery (1966)

After Rory Storm, and the decline of Merseybeat, the 21-year-old Hartley joined The Artwoods, a London-based band formed by Ronnie Wood's older brother Art Wood, in early 1965. The band never achieved sales to match their potential; also in the band was organist Jon Lord who was later in Deep Purple. Their 1966 album *Art Gallery* is a great showcase as to where British rock music was heading. After The Artwoods, Hartley joined John Mayall's Bluesbreakers and recorded *The Blues Alone* (it's just multi-instrumentalist Mayall and Hartley), *Crusade* and *Diary of a Band* with the legendary British blues player. Mick Taylor, who later joined the Stones, and John McVie of Fleetwood Mac

played in the Mayall band that recorded *Crusade*; and Taylor was still with the group for *Diary of a Band*, which was a double-album live recording.

Hartley was an extremely good drummer, with metronomic timing. You had to be good to play with John Mayall on whatever was your chosen instrument, and his leaving the band in 1968 to pursue his own musical direction was an amicable one, as is demonstrated by the spoof phone call on the start of The Keef Hartley Band's debut album *Halfbreed*, that came out in early 1969. The album strays little from the blues and jazz rock territory that Hartley was used to playing with his former boss, but benefits from the great blues singing of Miller Anderson and the excellent guitar playing of Ian Cruickshank; later Miller took over the guitarist's duties. Henry Lowther was a stalwart of the British jazz scene, having played with John Dankworth's Orchestra, while Jimmy Jewell was a jazz player at heart; he had spent a lot of time playing in soul and R&B groups. Gary Thain was a New Zealander who had arrived in London in 1968 as part of a trio called New Nadir, along with drummer Pete Dawkins and guitarist Ed Carter who later played with The Beach Boys for many years.

Halfbreed (1968)

"Woodstock was not as romantic as it has later been suggested. I am proud in a way to say I was a little part of it, but at the time it was a mess, mass confusion."

~ Miller Anderson

PERFORMANCE

The band's set included a medley from *Halfbreed* including the wonderful 'Just to Cry.' 'Believe in You' came from the band's second album *The Battle of Northwest Six* that the band recorded around the time of Woodstock.

"Deram Records got us on to the Woodstock festival. It all happened so fast. It was a new line-up of the Keef Hartley Band, and we were very under-rehearsed… We did not play well as we could not use our own equipment. We used Santana's gear. It was a missed chance for the band." ~ Miller Anderson

THE WOODSTOCK EFFECT

After their Woodstock appearance The Keef Hartley Band went on to make another five albums with a revolving cast of players. In fact it was very much in the jazz vein that they operated, with players coming and going, bringing with them new ideas and,

NOTTINGHAM'S 1969 POP & BLUES FESTIVAL
AT NOTTS. COUNTY FOOTBALL GROUND
ON SATURDAY, MAY 10th, from 12 noon to 11 p.m.
FLEETWOOD MAC
TREMELOES • MARMALADE
GEORGIE FAME•LOVE SCULPTURE•THE MOVE
PINK FLOYD • KEEF HARTLEY • STATUS QUO
DUSTER BENNETT • DREAM POLICE
VAN DER GRAAF GENERATOR
Presented by John Peel and Ed Stewart plus Dons Gear
Admission: 17/6 by ticket, 22/6 at gate. Block bookings of 25 or more at 15/-
Each available by postal application to:
STIRLING ENTERPRISES (NOTTINGHAM)
110 Grassington Road, Bobbers Mill, Nottingham

sometimes, a new direction. By their fifth album, *Seventy-Second Brave*, Anderson had left the band, and after that Keef went on to record a solo album called *Lancashire Hustler*. The only album to achieve any chart success was 1970s *The Time Is Near*, which made No. 41 in Britain. After doing session work, Keef set-up a joinery and cabinet making business, working for many top British recording studios making bespoke furniture for their studios. He did make the occasional solo appearance, but is now happily retired and living in his family home in Preston, Lancashire. Miller Anderson played with Spencer Davis for many years, recorded with T-Rex and is still playing. Gary Thain joined Uriah Heep after the Hartley band split but sadly died of a heroin overdose in 1975, aged 27.

45-MINUTE SET

SET LIST
'Spanish Fly'
'Believe In You'
'Rock Me Baby'
Medley:
'Leavin' Trunk'
'Halfbreed'
'Just To Cry'
'Sinnin' For You'

THE BAND
Keef Hartley - Drums
Miller Anderson - Guitar, Vocals
Jimmy Jewell - Saxophone
Henry Lowther - Trumpet, Violin
Gary Thain - Bass

The Incredible String Band at Woodstock. Left to right: Robin Williamson, Christina 'Licorice' McKechnie, Mike Heron and Rose Simpson

STRING BAND

The 5000 Spirits... (1967)

A STRANGE CHOICE of band to appear at the festival, especially having to follow The Keef Hartley Band and Santana; Woodstock wanted to rock not gaze at their collective navel. Robin Williamson and Clive Palmer were a duo popular on the Edinburgh folk scene in 1963, which is where they were spotted in 1965 by producer Joe Boyd; soon a third member was added by the name of Mike Heron who had a rock background. Boyd signed them to Elektra Records the following year and they recorded their eponymous first album. Soon after, Palmer left, leaving the two of them to carry on without him. The second album *The 5000 Spirits or The Layers of the Onion* came out in

TheHangman's Beautiful Daughter (1968)

1967 and received plaudits from everyone; Paul McCartney made it his 'album of the year'.

1968 had them release two new albums, *The Hangman's Beautiful Daughter* and *Wee Tam and The Big Huge*. They also added two new members, Licorice McKechnie and Rose Simpson, who also happened to be Robin and Mike's girlfriends. They were the embodiment of the hippie idyll and performed across America at the Fillmore's East and West, played festivals in the U.K. and appeared at the Royal Albert Hall, but they were one of those bands that you either got or dismissed instantly.

"We were told it was a little upstate folk festival."
~ Robin Williamson

PERFORMANCE
The Incredible String Band is one of those bands that you have to ask yourself, what on Earth were they doing at Woodstock? While the audience wanted heavy rock they got psychedelic folk-rock noodling.

THE WOODSTOCK EFFECT
After Woodstock the band set up a commune-style base in the south of Scotland and embarked upon an ill-conceived tour in 1970 in support of a performance piece called *U*. After debuting at London's Roundhouse, it closed after just a few performances at the Fillmore East in New York. It marked the beginning of a long, slow decline in fortunes for the band. The band signed to Island Records for the next five albums; Rose Simpson left after the first one and Licorice McKechnie departed a year later. Others joined the band, but it was never the same. Later both Williamson and Heron followed solo paths before getting back together in 1999 for the return of the ISB; it eventually ground to a complete halt in 2006 after Williamson had left in 2003.

40-MINUTE SET

SET LIST
'Invocation – Sleepers Awake'
'The Letter'
'This Moment Is Different'
'When You Find Out Who You Are'
Probably others

THE BAND
Mike Heron - Piano, Vocals
Robin Williamson - Guitar, Vocals
Christina 'Licorice' McKechnie - Percussion, Vocals
Rose Simpson - Bass, Vocals

SATURDAY
16 AUGUST

← GROOV

GE
HI

Canned Heat, with Bob 'The Bear' Hite in white shirt

CANNED HEAT

THE FACT THAT CANNED HEAT APPEARED at Woodstock was a matter of luck, and the gentle art of persuasion. Henry Vestine, the former Mothers Of Invention guitarist, quit just two days before the festival gig following a fight with bass player Larry Taylor at the Fillmore West. Harvey Mandel was drafted into the band only to find that drummer Adolpho 'Fito' de la Parra felt they didn't have sufficient time to rehearse for Woodstock, so he also left the band. Their manager got into the reluctant drummer's room where he had locked himself in, and talked him into changing his mind; they flew to Woodstock by helicopter, arriving in the nick of time. It was Harvey Mandel's third gig with the band; as they played, day turned to night and they had secured a prime slot on the already late-running second day.

Originally formed in 1965 as a jug band, they took their name from Tommy Johnson's 'Canned Heat Blues.' Their first incarnation was would-be disc jockey Bob 'The Bear' Hite who hailed from Torrance, California, Bostonian Al 'Blind Owl' Wilson, Frank Cook and Henry Vestine from Washington. Their original bass player was Stuart Brotman who later emerged in the U.S. band Kaleidoscope, alongside David Lindley. He was soon replaced by Mark Andes (who later co-founded Spirit), before New Yorker Samuel Larry Taylor came in as permanent bassist; he had served his apprenticeship with the likes of Chuck Berry and Jerry Lee Lewis, as well as playing on several of The Monkees hits. In 1967 the group signed to Liberty Records after appearing at the Monterey Pop Festival. In July 1967 they released a self-titled

album that made No. 76 on the album chart, following it with *Boogie With Canned Heat* in 1968, which spent three months on the *Billboard* chart. *Living the Blues*, a double album, came out in 1968 after which came *Hallelujah* in 1969, just before their Woodstock appearance.

Boogie With Canned Heat (1968)

"Technically, Vestine and Wilson are quite possibly the best two-guitar team in the world and Wilson has certainly become our finest white blues harmonica man. Together with powerhouse vocalist Bob Hite, they performed the country and Chicago blues idiom of the 1950s so skillfully and naturally that the question of which race the music belongs to becomes totally irrelevant." ~ *Down Beat* magazine, following their Monterey appearance

SATURDAY 16 AUGUST

'On the Road Again'
(1968)

In 1968 Cook had been replaced by de la Parra, who hailed from Mexico City, and it was soon after this that the band began to have hits with their unique blues sound. 'On The Road Again' went to No. 16 in the U.S. in the late summer of 1968, while Al Wilson's 'Going Up The Country' peaked at No. 11 in the US early in 1969. In the spring of '69 'Time Was' went to No. 67 on the *Billboard* charts. The band were also very popular in Britain where 'On The Road Again' went Top 10 and 'Going Up The Country' Top 20.

60-MINUTE SET

SET LIST
'Going Up The Country'
'A Change Is Gonna Come'
'Leaving This Town'
'I'm Her Man'
'Let's Work Together'
'Too Many Drivers At The Wheel'
'I Know My Baby'
'Woodstock Boogie'
'On The Road Again'

THE BAND
Bob 'The Bear' Hite - Vocals, Harmonica
Harvey 'The Snake' Mandel - Guitar
Alan 'Blind Owl' Wilson - Guitar, Harmonica, Vocals
Larry 'The Mole' Taylor - Bass
Adolpho 'Fito' de la Parra - Drums

PERFORMANCE

'Going Up The Country' became something of an unofficial theme song from the festival after it was featured in the movie. Coupled with 'On The Road Again,' which the band played as an encore, it helped catapult the band to even greater recognition. 'Woodstock Boogie' was very much a jam lasting close to 15 minutes, including the obligatory drum solo; it was a reworking of 'Fried Hockey Boogie' from *Boogie With Canned Heat*.

THE WOODSTOCK EFFECT

In September 1970, Al Wilson was found dead from a barbiturates overdose in Bob Hite's Topanga Canyon garden. He had suffered from depression and his

"The Woodstock performance which, although there were a couple of tunes which weren't too good, 'Going Up The Country' was one of them, there were some which were killers, stone killers."
~ Bob 'The Bear' Hite

death robbed the world of "the most gifted harmonica player I've ever heard," as John Lee Hooker described him. The band had been working with the blues legend on an album that became *Hooker 'n' Heat*. The following month 'Let's Work Together' from *Hallelujah* reached No. 26 on the *Billboard* chart, become their last single of any note; it reached No. 2 in the U.K.

By the mid-Seventies only Vestine, who had returned to the fold, and Hite remained of the original line up. The 294-pound Bob Hite died on 6 April 1981, which ended that chapter in the band's history. The band somehow carried on with Taylor and de la Parra, guitarist Junior Watson (late of The Mighty Flyers) and Walter Trout. By the time the band featured on John Lee Hooker's album *The Healer* in 1989, Vestine had rejoined the group yet again. Vestine died in October 1997 in a hotel outside Paris, France from heart and respiratory failure. He wanted his ashes to be scattered in a crater on the dark side of the Moon named after his father, a noted astrophysicist. Some of Canned Heat's longevity can be put down to their material regularly being featured in advertising campaigns on both sides of the Atlantic, which have included General Motors, Miller Beer, Levi's, Pepsi and 7-Up.

Leslie West onstage at Woodstock, 16 August 1969

MOUNTAIN

MOUNTAIN, before it was a group, was the title of Leslie West's 1969 solo album produced by Felix Pappalardi. By the time of Woodstock the 29-year-old bass-playing Pappalardi was an experienced session musician and producer; much of the credit for Mountain's success should be given to him. He was the son of a doctor from the Bronx and trained as a classical musician at the University of Michigan before drifting into the happening early Sixties Greenwich Village folk scene. He began working as a studio musician in 1963, working with among others Fred Neil and Tom Paxton; later he played bass for Tim Hardin and arranged for Buffy Saint-Marie, and by 1967 he was working as a producer for The Youngbloods.

Disraeli Gears   (1967)

Pappalardi's next production assignment was for Cream, the trio featuring Eric Clapton, Jack Bruce and Ginger Baker. He produced their second album *Disraeli Gears* (it takes its name from the popular, at the time, racing cycle gears, derailleur gears), which Cream recorded at Atlantic Studios in New York in May 1967. Featuring 'Sunshine of Your Love' and 'Strange Brew' (with lyrics by Pappalardi's wife Gail) it was a big hit in both Britain and America, going Top 5 in both countries, and gained the former bass-playing

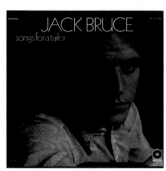

Songs For A Tailor   (1969)

folkie instant recognition and great kudos. In the following two years Felix produced Cream's *Wheels of Fire* as well as playing on it; then in October 1968 he produced Cream's *Goodbye Cream* album that was recorded live at the Forum in Los Angeles.

Following the break-up of Cream, Pappalardi produced Jack Bruce's outstanding first solo album, *Songs For a Tailor*, which included 'Theme For an Imaginary Western' that became a stand-out song for Mountain. After

Felix Pappalardi and Gail Collins' wedding, with guest Jack Bruce

"The thing Leslie and Eric have in common is lyricism; the ability to play a solo beautiful." ~ Felix Pappalardi

Mountain   (1969)

working with Bruce, Pappalardi began working with Leslie West who had been a member of The Vagrants, one of the few groups to come out of Manhattan. Leslie's brother played bass for The Vagrants, and Felix had produced some sides for them. They had a couple of minor regional R&B influenced hits in 1966 and 1967 but by the time Felix began working with West on his solo album the direction he was heading was territory more akin to Cream. West's solo album, *Mountain*, got released in early 1969 and featured Pappalardi on bass and N.D. Smart on drums (he was from Bo Grumpus, another band produced by Felix). It sounded a lot like the recently-disbanded British band.

60-MINUTES SET

SET LIST
Blood of the Sun
Stormy Monday
Theme for an Imaginary Western
Long Red
Who Am I But You and the Sun
Beside the Sea
Waiting to Take You Away
Dreams of Milk and Honey
Blind Man
Dirty Shoes Blues
Southbound Train

THE BAND
Leslie West - Guitar, Vocals
Felix Pappalardi - Bass
Norman D. Smart II - Drums
Steve Knight - Organ

"My whole concept of Mountain was to put Leslie out there. . . Our mutual admiration for each other brought us together and it's really happening." ~ Felix Pappalardi

They decided to form a touring band and in an effort to enhance the somewhat restrictive sound of

guitar, bass and drums they added keyboard player Steve Knight. Prior to playing Woodstock, Mountain had played just three gigs, so it's a testament to their musicianship that they pulled it off.

PERFORMANCE

Woodstock Two   (1971)

As this was only the band's fourth time together on stage it was a strong set with some great dynamics in the playing of Leslie West and the experienced Felix Pappalardi. Mountain had a good spot on the show, helped by having the same agent as Jimi Hendrix. 'Theme for an Imaginary Western' and 'Blood of the Sun' appear on the *Woodstock Two* album, but neither of the songs was recorded at Woodstock. Jack Bruce and Pete Brown wrote 'Theme for an Imaginary Western' and its similarity to many of Bruce's Cream songs is unmistakable; it became something of a signature song for Mountain. With the exception of 'Theme for an Imaginary Western' and the traditional blues song 'Stormy Monday' the majority of the set was taken from Leslie West's album entitled *Mountain*, which came out in 1969. Following on from *Dreams of Milk and Honey*, West performed one of what would become his trademark guitar solos.

"We weren't in the movie. I think our manager wanted too much money. I never forgot that, because I saw what it did for Ten Years After. I was so p*ssed off." ~ Leslie West

whaling trip) and it went one place higher than its predecessor. In 1973 *Flowers of Evil* was a minor, short-lived, hit on the album chart. In Britain *Nantucket Sleighride* was a very modest hit, as was their live album *The Road Goes Ever On*. In 1972 Mountain were no more and, ironically, out of its ashes West, Bruce and Laing formed, with the old Cream bassist. They recorded two studio albums and a live album before West and Pappalardi reformed Mountain in 1974, recording a studio as well as a live album; neither had any significant chart success. And that appeared to be it from a band that never really reached the heights that perhaps should have.

Nantucket Sleighride (1971)

In 1983 Pappalardi was shot by his wife Gail in their New York City apartment; she was charged with criminally negligent homicide and served a few years in jail. Pappalardi who had continued to produce sporadically since the end of Mountain, also failed to fulfill what some saw as the potential he showed during his work with Cream. Two years after Pappalardi's death, West and Laing took Mountain back on the road and into the studio and they have continued working ever since, most recently touring with Joe Satriani. 'Mississippi Queen' remains a staple of American rock radio and reminds us all of the brilliance of Leslie West's guitar playing.

THE WOODSTOCK EFFECT
Soon after Woodstock, Smart was replaced by Canadian drummer, Laurence 'Cory' Laing, and this was the line-up that went into the studio to record *Climbing* which was released in March 1970. From the album came the band's only significant hit single, 'Mississippi Queen' which reached No. 21 in America; the album itself got as high as No. 17 and also contained a nod to Woodstock in the song 'For Yasgur's Farm.'

The following year Mountain released the wonderfully named *Nantucket Sleighride* (it refers to a

THE GRATEFUL DEAD

FOR THE DEAD Woodstock was a gig that none of them enjoyed, and they probably wished they had stayed nearer to home than make the long trek east. With confusion over timings, who was going on stage when, the band had only just dropped acid and were in no fit state to play – and this was a band that were more used to being under the influence than most. All, that is, except Tom Constanten, who was not known to take acid.

"It was probably the worst set we've ever performed. Some people made their careers at Woodstock; we've spent about 20 years making up for it."
~ Bob Weir

Today the Grateful Dead's legend is so well formed that it's perhaps difficult to recall a time when they were just another popular West Coast band who were working and playing their way (mostly) in and around America's West in the company of the Airplane, The Doors, The Steve Miller Band, Quicksilver Messenger Service et al. The Dead had arisen from a jug band who had morphed into The Warlocks in early 1964 before becoming Grateful that another band were already recording as The Warlocks. They picked their name from a dictionary, although there's debate as to which particular dictionary it was, and their original line-up

was Jerry Garcia, Bob Weir, Phil Lesh, Bill Kreutzmann and Ron 'Pigpen' McKernan.

More than any of their contemporaries, the Dead have come to represent everything that was central to those who espoused the philosophy of a 'counter-culture.' For many it is this that first attracted them the band's music and was central to what the band were all about. This extended into the free-form nature of their performances that were, for many fans, more important than their official recordings.

The original Grateful Dead: Phil Lesh, Bill Kreutzmann, Jerry Garcia, Bob Weir and Ron 'Pigpen' McKernan

Jerry Garcia on stage with the Dead at Woodstock, 16 August 1969

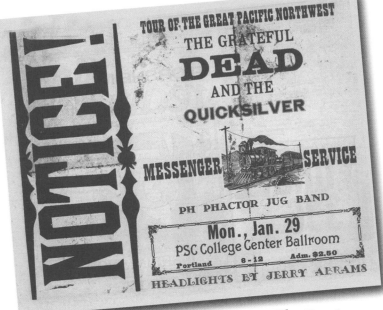

The Dead were less concerned with working out precisely what they were going to play than where, while getting into the mind-set to perform their long rambling sets that have come to epitomize the band. As early as 1966, Garcia was saying, "We don't make up our sets beforehand. We'd rather work off the tops of our heads than off a piece of paper."

Their first album, *The Grateful Dead,* was recorded in 1967 after the band signed to Warner Brothers; it was produced by The Rolling Stones' engineer Dave Hassinger in Los Angeles and took four days to make. It was essentially cut-down versions of their live shows and included a number of blues songs

Anthem of the Sun (1968)

including 'Viola Lee Blues,' which was one of the few that actually sounded much like the Dead played it on stage; it was over 10 minutes long, which was probably the reason that it sounded more authentic. It made No. 37 on the American album charts.

The following year the band released *Anthem of the Sun,* which they had spent around six months recording from the fall of 1967. It was the first Dead album to feature their second drummer, Mickey Hart, and is for many one of the high spots of the band's official

Aoxomoxoa (1969)

recorded output – despite this it only reached No. 87. Two months before Woodstock they released *Aoxomoxoa* which, like their set at the festival, opened with 'St. Stephen.' It also featured Tom Constanten who had officially joined the band after helping out on *Anthem of the Sun.* As they went on stage at Woodstock, *Aoxomoxoa* had struggled to No. 73 on the album chart and would go no higher. Not that any of the Dead were probably that bothered, their ethos was never anything much to do with record sales. The majority of the Dead's set were songs that they did not record on their official releases, although 'St. Stephen,' 'Dark Star,' 'Turn on Your Lovelight' all turned up on their *Live/Dead* album which came out three months after Woodstock, having been recorded at various gigs around America during the first half of the year – notably not at Woodstock.

"(There were) blue balls of electricity bouncing across the stage and into my guitar when I touched the strings."

~ Jerry Garcia, even after the stage had been dried.

PERFORMANCE

Exactly when the Dead went on stage is uncertain. After Mountain had cleared the stage the Dead's roadies took a good deal of time to get the band's equipment into position, because it was so heavy that it mangled the turntable mechanism designed to speed up the changeover of bands. Then Owsley Stanley, the LSD chemist and the Dead's soundman, was unhappy that the stage was wet and wanted it dried and grounded so none of the band would get electrocuted. So their 10.30pm start time may have been nearer 11.00pm. They started with 'St. Stephen' which segued into Merle Haggard's 'Mama Tried' followed by 'High Time' which petered out due to some equipment problems, which necessitated some long, drawn-out stage chat before the Dead continued with their set. It all ended around midnight with a lengthy version of "Turn on Your Lovelight'; at 40 minutes it was one of the longest versions of the song they ever did.

There was, of course, nothing unusual in the length of time the Dead played, nor the fact there were equipment failures – it was not the first, nor the last, time such things happened. What was unusual was that the Dead were not that great on an occasion

"It's nice to know that you can blow the most important gig of your career and it really doesn't matter." ~ Jerry Garcia, as he left the stage

when they had their largest-ever audience. However, there are many Deadheads who claim that while the band were not at their best, they were not that bad either; in the land of the Dead it's known as reverse mythologizing. You can listen to their show in streaming audio on the web and make up your own mind.

THE WOODSTOCK EFFECT

The Dead were one of the few bands that played at Woodstock whose appearance had little or no effect

90-MINUTE SET

SET LIST
St. Stephen
Mama Tried
High Time
Dark Star
High Time
Turn On Your Lovelight

THE BAND
Jerry Garcia - Guitar, Vocals
Bob Weir - Guitar, Vocals
Phil Lesh - Bass
Bill Kreutzmann - Drums, Percussion
Mickey Hart - Drums, Percussion
Ron 'Pigpen' McKernan - Organ, Vocals
Tom Constanten - Keyboards, Vocals

"Audiences are where it's at. That's what playing is all about. It's between the musicians and the audiences; it gives us somebody to work against." ~ Jerry Garcia, August 1966

on their future career. Would there have been more 'Deadhead' stickers on Cadillacs if they had appeared in the movie? Probably not. Such was the quality of their performance that it's doubtful if they would have given permission for it to have been used in the film. However, when Martin Scorsese came to edit their performance, possibly for his own use, as he was a fan, he found the light levels were so low that the footage was unusable; a case of heard and not seen.

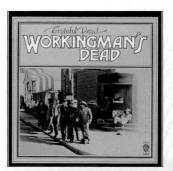

Workingman's Dead
(1970)

While the Dead were never an overtly commercial band, in 1970 they did well with *Workingman's Dead* which got to No. 27 on the album chart and then later in the year *American Beauty* reached No. 30. Over the next two years, two live albums did well. By the time of the eighth studio album, *Blues For Allah*, they had almost conquered the giddy heights of the Top 10 when it made No. 12 in late 1975. It wouldn't be until 1987 that they finally achieved their highest chart position when *In the Dark* made No. 6 – but you have to wonder if any of the band celebrated.

It was all part of the band's maturing sound that was as ever honed by playing live (the Dead

recorded many of their shows, and many of these recordings have appeared for sale both officially and unofficially).

In 1995 Jerry Garcia died. He was the band's de facto leader, although he hated to be called that, and so the band disbanded after 30 years and over 2,300 live shows.

Blues For Allah
(1975)

Since 1995, various formations of former Dead members have performed as The Other Ones, Phil Lesh and Friends, Rat Dog, and the Dead – this was a name change for The Other Ones. In February 2008 Mickey Hart, Phil Lesh, and Bob Weir, along with other musicians, performed as Deadheads for Obama.

125

CREEDENCE CLEARWATER REVIVAL

CREEDENCE CLEARWATER REVIVAL were one of the few bands at Woodstock to have had significant success on the *Billboard* charts, yet many people today probably don't even know that they actually appeared on the bill, because they did not feature in the movie or on the album. Their hour-long set was like a greatest hits album, with 'Bad Moon Rising' and 'Proud Mary' both having reached No. 2 on

the *Billboard* charts. As they walked on stage just after midnight on Saturday their current record, 'Green River,' was at No. 15, it's third week on the American chart; it would be their third single to stall at No. 2.

"By the time we got to Woodstock, I felt we were the number one band. Assuming that The Beatles were God, I thought that we were the next thing under them."
~ John Fogerty

To the band, Woodstock must have seemed like just another festival, although they were used to going on stage a little closer to their scheduled time. In the summer of '69 they had already played the Newport Festival in California, the Denver and the Atlanta festivals, along with the Atlantic City Festival that summer. They were just about the hottest band on the charts, if success is measured in the number of singles that they had already sold.

John and Tom Fogerty, Doug Clifford and Stu Cook first recorded in 1964 as The Golliwogs; Tom Fogerty worked as a packing clerk in San Francisco at Fantasy Records, a jazz label. Fantasy released 'Don't Tell Me No Lies,' sung by Tom, in late 1964, but neither it nor the 1965 follow-ups 'Where You

Green River (1969)

Been?' and 'You Can't Be True,' were played on the radio outside of their local area. They were just another Bay Area bar band until 'Brown-Eyed Girl' sold 10,000 copies in California and adjoining states. It looked likely that they would stay that way because both John Fogerty and Doug Clifford were drafted into the Army.

In 1967 John finished his stint in the army and the band picked up where they had left off, beginning by renaming themselves as CCR. There are competing stories as to how it happened; it may have been the name of one of Tom Fogerty's friends or it could have come from a beer commercial. 'Suzie Q' was their first single in 1968; 'I Put a Spell On You' followed it. Both cover versions were on the band's first album, which reached No. 52 on the *Billboard* chart. Despite their success they never could break into the 'inner circle' of San Francisco bands like Jefferson Airplane and the Dead, which annoyed John Fogerty no end. In May 1968 they made their Avalon Ballroom debut on a bill with Taj Mahal; two months later they played the Fillmore West with the Paul Butterfield Blues Band. With 'Suzie Q' on the *Billboard* chart they played the Fillmore West three more times on bills with Fleetwood Mac and Jethro Tull.

"We'd done an Andy Williams TV Special the night before and we didn't get out of LA until midnight." ~ Doug Clifford

Maybe they were outsiders in San Francisco but they were at the top of their game when they played Woodstock. John Fogerty's unique voice and great songwriting had come together as a perfect combination just at the right time.

"We were supposed to be in the prime spot for that evening. The Dead went on and pulled their usual shenanigans." ~ John Fogerty

PERFORMANCE

The band played their current single and their two previous No. 2s very much as they were on record. As the set progressed they stretched their songs out into longer, more improvized, rock songs, which was their normal way of playing them. It also included a cover of 'Ninety-nine and a Half,' a Wilson Pickett song they recorded for their debut album. 'I Put A Spell On You' stretched the 5-minute single to almost twice its length, while 'Keep On Chooglin'' ran for close to ten minutes. 'Suzie Q', the Dale Hawkins classic, had been their first hit and on the album it ran for eight minutes; for their encore they kept it rocking for even longer.

60-MINUTE SET

SET LIST
Born On The Bayou
Green River
Ninety-Nine And A Half (Won't Do)
Commotion
Bootleg
Bad Moon Rising
Proud Mary
I Put A Spell On You
Night Time Is The Right Time
Keep On Chooglin'
Suzie Q

THE BAND
John Fogerty – Lead guitar, Vocals
Tom Fogerty – Rhythm guitar, Vocals
Doug Clifford – Drums
Stu Cook – Bass

"I could never put my finger on what it was, but we were considered outsiders in our own town." ~ John Fogerty

THE WOODSTOCK EFFECT

If they are not remembered for their Woodstock appearance Creedence Clearwater Revival are far from forgotten around the world. Their music is a staple of oldies radio and their catalog of great records is still regularly repackaged and sells in large numbers. 'Green River,' like 'Bad Moon Rising' and 'Proud Mary,' also made No. 2 on the *Billboard* chart as did 'Travellin' Band' and 'Lookin' out My Back Door' in 1970, making them one of those unlucky bands that could never break through to achieve the coveted top spot on the American singles chart; they did top the charts in Britain with 'Bad Moon Rising.' Their album *Green River* came out a month after Woodstock and it topped the charts for four weeks, as did *Cosmo's Factory* following year, although it had a nine-week run at No. 1.

Cosmo's Factory (1970)

From there on the band's career went into a steady decline, with their last charting album coming in 1972 and their last *Billboard* hit single was in 1976 with 'I Heard It Through the Grapevine,' although this was taken from *Cosmo's Factory*.

By the time of their 1972 album, which *Rolling Stone* called "the worst album ever made by a major rock band," things were staring to fall apart. CCR were all about John Fogerty's brilliant songs and his soulful voice – he's the archetypical 'rock vocalist.'

Mardi Gras (1972)

Put him into almost any great rock band of the Sixties and Seventies and he would have at least held his own as their lead singer and more often as not improved upon what they did. Handing over joint creative control of the band to the other three members might have been the decent thing to do, but it was a creative disaster. Then again, John Fogerty and the others may have just run their creative course; the band officially disbanded in October 1972. John Fogerty pursued a solo career, although he refused to perform any CCR hits until 1987, when both Dylan and George Harrison told him everyone would think 'Proud Mary' is Tina Turner's song unless he did them. 'Rockin' All Over The World,' which Status Quo recorded in 1977 and took to No. 3 in the UK charts, turning it into their own 'anthem', came from John Fogerty's second solo album.

John's brother Tom died of TB in 1990 after contracting AIDS following a blood transfusion; sadly he died without ever reconciling with John after the band's acrimonious break-up. Cook and Clifford worked for various bands before forming Creedence Clearwater Revisited, which landed them in court with John Fogerty; the drummer and bassist eventually won the right to use the name.

Creedence Clearwater Revival in London in April 1970. Left to right: Tom Fogerty, Doug Clifford, John Foggarty and Stu Cook

Janis Joplin at Woodstock, 17 August 1969

JANIS JOPLIN

JANIS JOPLIN, the 26-year-old powerhouse blues singer, was another casualty of the late-running Saturday show that just kept on getting later the longer it went on. Born in Port Arthur, Texas, the daughter of a Texaco engineer, Janis came under the influence of Bessie Smith, Leadbelly and Odetta from listening to their records while in her early teens. While she was still at the University of Texas in 1962, the campus newspaper ran a story about the 19-year-old student saying that "she dared to be different."

"They put me down, man, those square people in Port Arthur. And I wanted them so much to love me."
~ Janis Joplin

Janis failed to complete her course and by 1964 she had drifted to San Francisco and was living in Haight Ashbury, where she recorded some songs with a guitarist named Jorma Kaukonen who would later join Jefferson Airplane. Among the songs were several old blues standards, which would be a feature of her output ever after. As well as singing the blues, she, like many of her heroines (and heroes) was attracted to drink and drugs, and it was during these early years in San Francisco that she acquired a reputation for being a hard-living woman who lived a life that mirrored the songs she sang. By mid 1965 she had been persuaded to return to Port Arthur, where for a while she adopted a more sober life style; she even got engaged to a man who by all accounts

was extremely respectable – a least he wore a suit.

By mid-1966 Janis was back in San Francisco, having been persuaded to move there by Chet Helms, who she knew from Texas and who was managing a band named Big Brother & the Holding Company. They had begun life as a four-piece back in January '66. Peter Albin (bass), Sam Andrew (guitar), James Gurley (guitar) and Chuck Jones (drums) were the original members, but by the time Janis joined, Dave Getz had replaced Jones.

Having spent several weeks in Chicago in August 1966 working at a club, which was none too successful, the band returned to San Francisco and moved into a house with the Grateful Dead. For the rest of the year and into the early part of 1967, Big Brother played up and down the West Coast, appearing regularly at the Fillmore, the Winterland and Avalon Ballroom in San Francisco. Then in June 1967 they got what would prove to be their big break when they appeared at the Monterey Pop Festival; shortly afterwards they also acquired a new manager who got them a deal with Columbia Records

"Big Brother & the Holding Company was a prime example of a band where the chemistry was right, where the whole was greater than the sum of its parts."
~ Sam Andrew

Cheap Thrills (1968)

Before anything could happen with Columbia, Mainstream Records released an album recorded back in December 1966. It did moderately well on the album charts for a band with little of a following outside of the West Coast, peaking at No. 60 on the charts. They recorded *Cheap Thrills*, their first Columbia album, between March and May 1968 and it was released in August to considerable acclaim. With its distinctive cover art by Robert Crumb, its sound is raw and powerful and includes a 10-minute version of 'Ball and Chain.' By October 1968 it had made No. 1 on the U.S. album chart helped by the fact that 'Piece Of My Heart' got to No. 12 on the *Billboard* singles chart – by the end of the year it had sold close to a million copies.

60-MINUTE SET

SET LIST
Raise Your Hand
As Good As You've Been To This World
To Love Somebody
Summertime
Try (Just A Little Bit Harder)
Kozmic Blues
I Can't Turn You Loose
Work Me Lord
Piece Of My Heart
Ball And Chain

THE BAND
Janis Joplin – Vocals
John Till - Guitar
Maury Baker - Drums
Brad Campbell – Bass
Cornelius Flowers - Baritone Sax, Vocals
Luis Gasca – Trumpet
Terry Clements - Tenor Sax
Richard Kermode - Keyboards

"Sex is the closest I can come to explaining it, but it's more than sex. I get stoned from happiness. I want to do it until it isn't there any more." ~ Janis Joplin, August 1968

"Janis asked me to play Woodstock, but I was worn out, felt that I had done my duty and left for California about two weeks before the event. Now I wish I would have played the Festival, just so that I could have played at the beginning, Monterey, and the end, Woodstock." ~ Sam Andrew

By the end of 1968 Janis had left Big Brother in search of her own thing; she formed a new backing band, The Kozmic Blues Band. During this time it's alleged that she was spending $200 every day to support her heroin habit. Shortly before she appeared at Woodstock she completed recording her debut solo album, *I Got Them Ol' Kozmic Blues Again Mama!* On the album is most of the band that appeared with Janis at Woodstock, although her former Big Brother band mate, Sam Andrew, who plays on it, had already moved on.

I Got Them Ol' Kozmic Blues Again Mama! (1969)

PERFORMANCE
Janis Joplin was another artist who was not at her best by the time she got on stage, having had to hang around for hours waiting to go on. Too much booze, too many drugs and tiredness were all factors in

Janis Joplin with Big Brother & the Holding Company at Winterland, San Fancisco, 1967

Janis Joplin at Woodstock, 17 August 1969

"Are you staying stoned? Have you got enough water and everything?"

~ Janis Joplin just before she sings 'Work Me Lord' at Woodstock

making her Woodstock appearance patchy at best. Much of her material was taken from her *I Got Them Ol' Kozmic Blues Again Mama!* album. Her two encore songs, 'Piece of My Heart' and 'Ball and Chain' were from *Cheap Thrills*. Her opener, 'Raise Your Hand,' was written by soul singer and Stax stalwart Eddie Floyd, and 'Work Me Lord' is a traditional song on which Janis gives one of the best performances of her set. 'I Can't Turn You Loose' is sung by Cornelius Flowers with Janis just singing backing vocals.

"These kids who touch drugs are crazy when they can have a drink of Southern Comfort."

~ Janis Joplin, February 1970

THE WOODSTOCK EFFECT

Following her appearance at Woodstock, Joplin and The Kozmic Blues Band were back on the road. According to Sam Andrew, "Janis and a group of very drunk people, including the fabulous Buddy Guy, took a train trip across Canada, the Festival Express. I don't miss having played at Woodstock, but I very much miss that train trip." They played throughout the U.S.A. as well in support of her record, which eventually managed to make No. 5 on the American album charts helped by the single

Pearl (1971)

'Kozmic Blues,' which got to No. 41 as she and her backing band were breaking up at New York's Madison Square Garden just before Christmas 1969. After taking some time away from music in the first part of 1970, Janis put together The Full Tilt Boogie Band while also taking time out to appear at a couple of gigs with the reformed Big Brother & the Holding Company.

During the early summer she toured with her band and appeared on *The Dick Cavett Show* before appearing at a gig at Harvard Stadium in Boston on 12 August; it was to be her last stage appearance. In September Janis and her band were in Los Angeles working on an album, and on 3 October she was at the studio working on some tracks. The following day she was found dead in her hotel room; the official cause of her death was an overdose of heroin. *Pearl*, the album she was making, came out in February 1971 and eventually topped the U.S. charts for nine weeks; 'Me and Bobby McGhee,' a single taken from *Pearl*, went to No.1 on the singles chart.

Her legacy is to have introduced many people to the blues, especially some of the great female blues singers she emulated in her music and in her lifestyle. She lived it like she sang it.

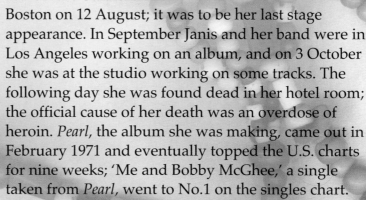

SLY & THE FAMILY STONE

SLY WAS BORN SYLVESTER STEWART in Dallas, Texas, in 1944, and he, along with his family, moved to California in the late 1950s. By 1961 he had a small local hit with 'A Long Time Alone' and by the mid Sixties he was working as a DJ on KDIA San Francisco, as well as producing records for Bobby Freeman, Grace Slick's first band, The Great Society, and The Beau Brummels. He formed Sly & The Family Stone in 1966, having initially had a band named The Stoners; this became the core of The Family Stone along with Sly's brother Freddie, sister Rosemary, cousin Larry Graham, Greg Errico, Cynthia Robinson and Jerry Martini. The band was a mixture of black and white, which was virtually unheard of outside of jazz circles in the mid Sixties.

The band harnessed a disparate musical melange of soul, rock, R&B, psychedelia and funk that was labelled 'Psychedelic Soul.' Their arrangements were clever, complex and rhythmic as well as having great

Dance To The Music
(1968)

pop melodies. Their debut single 'I Ain't Got Nobody' gained some local airplay, but their debut album *A Whole New Thing*, released in 1967, did nothing. The follow-up album's title cut changed everything. 'Dance to the Music' was a top 10 hit in both America and

> **"We all got together in the basement of Sly's house. It seemed like a little miracle the way we all got together: it was as if fate had a hand in the situation."**
> ~ Freddie Stone

Britain and was a ground-breaking single. The follow-up, 'M'Lady,' faltered at a disappointing No. 93 in America; the album from which it was taken also failed to chart.

In February 1969, the band released the wonderfully swinging 'Everyday People' that soared to No. 1 in the U.S.A. topping the charts for four weeks. 'Sing a Simple Song' and 'Stand' both made the *Billboard* charts in early 1969; all three songs came from the album *Stand!* The week before Woodstock, 'Hot Fun in The Summertime' entered the *Billboard* chart at No. 79; it was sitting at No. 54 when the band

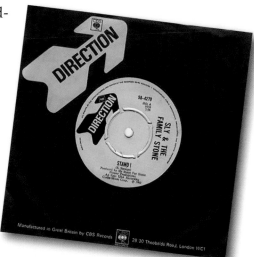

SUNDAY 17 AUGUST

141

Stand (1969)

went on stage – it made No. 2 in October.

PERFORMANCE

Against the odds, given how late it was before they went on, Sly & the Family Stone gave a standout performance, which was full of energy and great music. 'Music Lover' and 'I Want To Take You Higher' took up about a third of their hour-long set and the majority of the material was taken from the album *Stand* that was in the Top 20, having entered the *Billboard* album chart three months before Woodstock.

60-MINUTE SET

SET LIST
M'lady
Sing A Simple Song
You Can Make It If You Try
Everyday People
Dance To The Music
Music Lover
I Want To Take You Higher
Love City
Stand

THE BAND
Sly Stone - Vocals, Keyboard, Harmonica
Freddie Stone - Guitar, Vocals
Greg Errico - Drums
Larry Graham - Bass
Jerry Martini - Saxophone, Tambourine
Cynthia Robinson - Trumpet
Rosie Stone - Keyboard, Vocals, Tambourine

"Sly was playing his very happy and funky soul music and everybody was on their feet. Everybody in the amphitheater were standing and dancing or just bouncing up and down." ~ Critic Mike Jahn

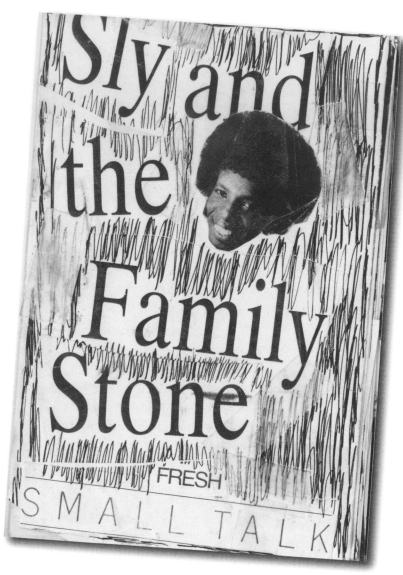

THE WOODSTOCK EFFECT

The 1970s started well for the band in America with their second No. 1, 'Thank You (Falettinme Be Mice Elf Agin),' followed later in the year by 'I Wanna Take You Higher' (No. 38). Their only hit of 1971 was the brilliant 'Family Affair', their third U.S. No. 1. Later in 1972 they released 'Runnin' Away'; both the last two hits were taken from the band's U.S. No. 1 album *There's A Riot Goin' On*.

In 1973 the band started to run out of steam; although there were more hits, none were very big

There's A Riot Goin' On
(1972)

hits. The best of them was 'If You Want Me To Stay' that made No. 12. By this time Larry Graham had left the band to form Graham Central Station.

Stone's album *Fresh* was his last work of significance. It was around this time that he started to fall prey to severe drug addiction, which slowly sapped him of his prodigious talent. By the mid Seventies the Family Stone had broken up, Sly had filed for bankruptcy and his records were not selling. He reformed the Family Stone at the end of 1976 and they soldiered on until the end of the decade without having any hit records. In the early Eighties Sly worked briefly with George Clinton and then in 1984 Bobby Womack had Sly play on his U.S. tour after helping Sly kick his drug habit. Stone appeared on Jesse Johnson's 1986 lowly-placed hit 'Crazay' in 1987 and dueted with Martha Davis on 'Love & Affection' for the *Soul Man* soundtrack; he also he recorded a single 'Eek-a-Bo-Static,' but it did not chart.

By the end of the 1980s things became desperate for Stone. He was arrested in Connecticut for driving under the influence of cocaine, then a couple of months later he was sentenced to 14 months in rehab and put on probation for possessing cocaine. While he continued to battle his addiction he was

inducted into the Rock & Roll Hall of Fame in 1993; after appearing at the induction ceremony it was reported that he was living in a sheltered-housing scheme. Various incarnations of The Family Stone have appeared over the last 20 years and in 2007 Sly himself performed with the band but without great success.

Sly Stone was an original who did more than anyone to create the rock funk fusion of dance music in the 1980s and 1990s. His albums *There's A Riot Goin On* and *Stand* have both been hailed in recent years as groundbreaking. In retrospect it was Woodstock that helped the band to gain acceptance by many white rock fans where other black groups failed.

"The Family Stone always had a showmanship most other local bands couldn't muster. On the air Sly was the same. Sly didn't create an 'on-air' personality; that was Sly Stone." ~ Bill Doubleday, general manager at KDIA

THE WHO

THE FACT THAT THE WHO APPEARED AT ALL at Woodstock had a lot to do with their road manager John Wolff; he had the job of dealing with the organizers. He tackled John Morris about the delicate subject of money and was offered a check, but this was not going to satisfy the band – especially Pete Townshend. For a long while Morris avoided Wolff until it was practically time to go on, and then the organizers tried the old "Well, you'll have to go on." There was no budging Wolff, or The Who, so eventually a helicopter had to be dispatched to bring the money from the bank, having first picked up the manager because the vault was on a time lock. The Who got the remainder of their $11,200, having already been paid a deposit, and the public that were still awake got a great show.

Like many other bands that started out in Britain in the early Sixties, The Who traced their roots back to skiffle and early rock'n'roll. School friends John Entwistle and Pete Townshend were more jazz-influenced than most as they played in The Confederates, a trad jazz band. One day, Entwistle met Roger Daltrey in the street, and as John had his bass slung over his shoulder Roger wasted no time in inviting him along to a rehearsal of his band, The Detours. Six months later Pete Townshend was in The Detours as well, having been pitched as a "great rhythm guitar player" by Entwistle. The Fox & Goose in Ealing and the White Hart Hotel in Acton were typical Detours'

"At Woodstock people were so appalled when The Who asked for their money – having just traveled 7,000 miles to get there. I said to some guy, 'Listen, this is the f*ing American dream, it's not my dream. I don't want to spend the rest of my life in f***ing mud, smoking f***ing marijuana. If that's the American dream, let us have our f***ing money and p*ss off back to Shepherd's Bush where people are people."** ~ Pete Townshend

John Entwistle, Keith Moon and Pete Townshend at Woodstock, Sunday 17 August 1969

venues in early 1963, before they changed their name to The Who in early 1964 and acquired a new drummer, seventeen-year-old lunatic Keith John Moon. Soon afterwards The Who became The High Numbers, under the influence of their new publicist, Peter Meaden and released their first U.K. single in early summer 1964; 'I'm the Face' failed to chart.

After being discovered by their managers Kit Lambert and Chris Stamp in July, Pete Townshend accidentally smashed his first guitar at a gig at the Railway Hotel in Harrow. By November, they had reverted back to their original name of The Who. Also that month, American record producer Shel Talmy produced the first Who single, 'I Can't Explain,' which eventually reached No. 8 in the U.K. chart by April. There followed over the next few years a string of wonderful pop singles, most of which made the U.K. Top 10, including 'Anyway, Anyhow, Anywhere,' the classic 'My Generation,' which made No. 2 in late-'65, as did 'I'm A Boy'

America had marginally better taste than Britain when it came to The Who. 'I Can See For Miles' made No. 9 in the *Billboard* chart as 1967 was coming to an end. It was the biggest hit single The Who achieved in the U.S.A. – 'My Generation' had only made No. 74 and 'Happy Jack,' the previous best-performing song, had just failed to get into the *Billboard* Top 20. For most bands, before the *Pepper*-shed, singles were what counted and while The Who had done fairly well with the *My Generation* and *A Quick One* (known as *Happy Jack* in the US) albums in 1965 and '66 respectively, their first attempt at anything a little more adventurous, *The Who Sell Out,* only got to No. 13 in Britain in early 1968. In America their only album, prior to 1969, to achieve any success was a compilation, *Magic Bus – The Who On Tour,* which made No. 39 on the U.S. album chart.

Nothing that had gone before could have prepared their fans for what came next. *Tommy* was recorded between September 1968 and March 1969; it was released in May to critical and fan acclaim – in equal measure – although there were some poor misguided critics who deemed it 'sick.' Despite an initially poor sales start, the double album's growing mystique eventually pushed *Tommy* to No. 2 in Britain and No. 4 in America and formed the core of their Woodstock set. The story of the 'deaf, dumb

Tommy (1969)

in 1966 – The Who's highest U.K. singles chart placing. In 1967 The Who had two big British hit singles with 'Happy Jack' and 'Pictures Of Lily'; strangely one of their best records, 'I Can See For Miles' only made it to No. 10 in the U.K. in November '67. It's classic Who – showcasing every aspect of what made them the best rock band to come out of England – The Stones may have rocked and rolled; The Who just ROCKED.

Keith Moon, Roger Daltrey and Pete Townshend of The Who at Woodstock, Sunday 17 August 1969

and blind kid' was Pete Townshend's masterpiece as a writer and The Who's crowning glory as a band. At the time it was dubbed a 'rock opera' but as many have pointed out ever since it lacked the normal opera form. Whatever it is, it's a tour de force that was groundbreaking; rock has never been the same since.

70-MINUTE SET

SET LIST
Heaven And Hell
I Can't Explain
It's A Boy
1921
Amazing Journey
Sparks
Eyesight To The Blind
Christmas
Acid Queen
Pinball Wizard
Do You Think It's Alright?
Fiddle About
There's A Doctor I've Found
Go To The Mirror
Smash The Mirror
I'm Free
Tommy's Holiday Camp
We're Not Gonna Take It
See Me Feel Me
Summertime Blues
Shakin' All Over
My Generation / Naked Eye

THE BAND
Roger Daltrey - Vocals
Pete Townshend - Guitar, Vocals
John Entwistle - Bass, Vocals
Keith Moon - Drums

"The thing that saved us was the sun coming up. When I sang 'See Me, Feel Me' the sun peeked over the back of the crowd. It was the best light show we could ever have had." ~ Roger Daltrey

PERFORMANCE

As The Who's set was reaching its climax the sun was coming up. It was 6:05am on Sunday morning, not the ideal time for any band to perform at their best, but despite that, they were magnificent. Roger Daltrey in particular was in fine voice, which must have been hard having been waiting for so long to even get on stage. The Who's set was typical of their live performances at the time featuring a scaled-down version of *Tommy* along with some old hits and rock'n'roll numbers – Eddie Cochran's 'Summertime Blues' and Johnny Kidd and the Pirates' 'Shakin' All Over.'

During The Who's set there was a surprising incident when Abbie Hoffman decided to invade the stage just after they had played 'Pinball Wizard' and were about to start 'Do You Think It's Alright'; he got short shrift from Pete Townshend. As Pete was tuning up, Hoffman grabbed the microphone and started ranting about the imprisonment of John Sinclair, the leader of the White Panther Movement and the MC5's manager. Townshend was incensed Hoffman should have known better than to invade The Who's stage; Pete hit him with his guitar while herding him off the stage with a chorus of invective. When their set finished just how many people in the audience were awake to witness Pete's ritualistic bashing of his guitar goes unrecorded. Townshend finished by throwing it into the first rows of the crowd. According to some reports, a hapless roadie was despatched among the 400,000 to retrieve it!

THE WOODSTOCK EFFECT

Woodstock was the making of The Who's reputation in America. Their appearance helped to propel *Tommy* into the top 5 and then when *Live At Leeds*

The Who at Woodstock, Sunday 17 August 1969.

The Who at Woodstock, Sunday 17 August 1969.

Live At Leeds (1970)

came out a year later it, too, made No. 4 on the U.S. album charts, as did 1971's *Who's Next*. While none of their singles matched the success of 'I Can See For Miles' in the U.S.A. The Who did have the odd top ten single during the 1970s in Britain, but by this time they had become a fully-fledged rock band with singles no longer as important as such ambitious albums as 1973's *Quadrophenia*, the follow-up concept album to *Tommy*.

Just as they released the *Who Are You* album in 1978, tragedy struck when Keith Moon died in his sleep after taking an overdose of a prescription drug designed to help him combat his alcohol addiction. Kenney Jones, who had started in The Small Faces – he was still with them when they grew up and became The Faces – joined the band and was an able, if less inspiring, replacement. They continued with this line-up until 1983 when Townshend officially announced his departure from The Who.

After appearing at Live Aid in 1985, The Who were back on the road in 1989 for a 25th anniversary tour with Simon Phillips on drums; Townshend's hearing problems reduced him to acoustic guitar and it was not The Who fans had come to cherish.

Endless Wire (2006)

However, the tour did phenomenal business and included several performances of *Tommy* featuring guest stars including Billy Idol and Phil Collins. Through the 1990s various incarnations of the band took place, including one without Townshend,

although Daltrey refused to call it The Who, opting for 'Daltrey Sings Townshend' instead. By 1999 The Who were back as a five-piece with Ringo Starr's son Zak Starkey on drums and John 'Rabbit' Bundrick on keyboards – this was more like the classic Who of old.

Things looked set to continue when John Entwistle died in a Las Vegas hotel room from a heart attack, possibly brought on by the effects of cocaine, in 2002. Since then The Who have carried on with Pete and Roger finding renewed creative and performing energy. The Who are timeless, just like their music, much of which sounds as fresh today as when it was first recorded, which is more than can be said of many of their contemporaries.

"We don't want those long hiatuses that we used to have... You should at least keep the ball rolling."
~ Roger Daltrey, 2008

JEFFERSON AIRPLANE

IT WAS LONG BEFORE the Summer of Love that the nascent Jefferson Airplane got together in San Francisco. It was the summer of '65 when singer, and would-be pop star Marty Balin, who had already recorded a couple of singles, met folkie Paul Kantner. The two of them became the core of the house band for a club named The Matrix, along with Jorma Kaukonen and singer Signe Toly Anderson. By the

fall of 1965 the newly-named Jefferson Airplane, a name inspired by blues singer Blind Lemon Jefferson, had recruited Jack Casady on bass and Skip Spence on drums. The band got a real boost from early in their existence when music critic Ralph Gleason, who wrote the sleeve notes to Frank Sinatra's 1959 album *No One Cares*, said, they are "one of the best bands ever."

It was in late October that the Airplane, as they soon became known, were supported at a gig at San Francisco's Longshoremen's Hall by another local band, The Great Society, whose singer was Grace Slick. Within a month the Airplane had signed a deal with RCA and recorded their first single, the driving 'It's No Secret.' After recording their debut album, *Jefferson Airplane Takes Off*, Spence left the band and was replaced by Spencer Dryden in time for a 4th July show at the Berkeley Folk Festival; Spence later formed Moby Grape and wrote one of

SUNDAY 17 AUGUST

158

Jefferson Airplane and their audience of 400,000 at Woodstock, 17 August 1969

Grace Slick backstage at Woodstock, 17 August 1969

"If you can remember anything about the Sixties, you weren't really there." ~ Paul Kantner

the great guitar classics, 'Omaha.'

By the time that the first album came out in September Anderson had had a baby, and she left the band a month later after a gig at the Fillmore; the following night Slick joined and the classic Jefferson Airplane line-up was complete, the one that was still together three years later. By early 1967 Bill Graham became their manager and they had played the legendary Human Be-In that ushered in the Summer of Love. They also recorded their second album, *Surrealistic Pillow*, which reached No. 3 on the album chart; it included the band's two biggest hit singles, 'Somebody to Love' (No. 5) and 'White Rabbit' (No. 8). 'Somebody to Love' had originally been a B-side of a Great Society 45 and the Airplane's version was for many the ultimate evocation of the counterculture for the mainstream. The band's appearance at Monterey in June and in the film helped to spur international interest in their music.

Surrealistic Pillow (1967)

In November 1967 *After Bathing at Baxter's* made No. 17 on the album chart; it lacked the strong singles of its predecessor. The following year the *Crown of*

Creation album peaked at No. 6 on the U.S. album chart, it's success a testament to its musical strength in depth because it too had no defining singles to drive sales. Four months before Woodstock, the band went into Wally Heider's San Francisco studio to record their most political motivated album and a definite change of direction in sound. Besides its strong anti-war message, *Volunteers* also delved into ecology and generally positioned the band as one of the most thinking outfits in rock. It also featured British piano and keyboard virtuoso Nicky Hopkins, which is how he came to be with the band when they played Woodstock.

"Alright friends, you have seen the heavy groups, now you'll see morning maniac music, believe me. It's a new dawn." ~ Grace Slick as the band began their set

45-MINUTE SET

SET LIST
Somebody To Love
The Other Side Of This Life
Plastic Fantastic Lover
Volunteers
Won't You Try/ Saturday Afternoon
Eskimo Blue Day
Uncle Sam's Blues
White Rabbit

THE BAND
Marty Balin - Vocals
Grace Slick - Vocals
Paul Kantner - Guitar, Vocals
Jorma Kaukonen - Guitar, Vocals
Jack Casady - Bass
Spencer Dryden - Drums
Nicky Hopkins – Piano

PERFORMANCE

When Grace Slick sang the opening lines of 'White Rabbit' at Woodstock the audience were privileged to hear one of the great Sixties rock vocalists – she doesn't smoke, she smoulders. The set list is probably only some of what they played that day but unfortunately nobody was keeping detailed notes. At a concert the week before in New York's Central Park they also played 'The Ballad of You and Me and Pooneil,' 'Come Back Baby,' 'Fat Angel,' 'Wooden Ships,' '3/5 of a Mile in 10 Seconds,' 'We Can Be Together,' 'Feel So Good' and 'Mau Mau'.

THE WOODSTOCK EFFECT

Volunteers (1969)

Volunteers made No. 13 on the U.S. album chart as the year ended; it had entered the charts a week before the Airplane had played the Altamont Festival, the infamous concert headlined by The Rolling Stones near San Francisco. Two months later drummer Spencer Dryden quit, burned out from the acid-fueled hippy

"We were music gods."
~ Marty Balin

merry-go-round. By way of release, Kaukonen and Casady began working on a side project they called Hot Tuna; it was conceived to explore their love of traditional blues, which they have continued to do until the present day. Paul Kantner and Grace Slick,

"Woodstock was the high point of all the concerts and festivals. That was the beginning of what music can do politically and as a force."
~ Marty Balin

who started a relationship in 1970, explored a sci-fi musical direction with an album entitled *Blows Against the Empire*, which was released as Paul Kantner – Jefferson Starship. It included the cream of West Coast musicians; among them were, Jerry Garcia, David Crosby, the Airplane's new drummer Joey Covington and David Freiberg from Quicksilver Messenger Service.

Slick and Kantner's daughter China was born in January 1971, and two months later Marty Balin announced he was leaving the group he founded. He had begun to follow a much healthier lifestyle eschewing drugs and drink; it's said the death of his friend Janis Joplin pushed him farther along this path. After Grace Slick was almost killed in a car crash in May 1971 the band released their last RCA album, *Bark*; it was another that did surprisingly well considering a lack of obvious radio records. With internal squabbles and Slick's battle with drink the band just about managed to record one more album, *Long John Silver*. David Freiberg came in as vocalist and in September 1972 their shows at San Francisco's Winterland were their last.

In 1974 Jefferson Starship took flight, and a series of big-selling albums were released during the 1970s including *Red Octopus* which topped the charts in 1975, spawning the No. 3 single 'Miracles.' However, Grace Slick tarnished her reputation by becoming a drunken liability on stage and she finally left the band in 1978. She returned in 1981, then Kantner left in 1984 and the band renamed themselves Starship, scoring a massive hit with 'We Built This City' – the first No. 1 single by any incarnation of the Airplane / Starship franchise.

Slick stayed with the Starship until 1988 when she quit and joined the reformed Jefferson Airplane. This was the definitive line-up, minus Dryden, and after an album release and a moderately successful tour the band finally split. Kantner resurrected Jefferson Starship in the 1990s and they're still playing the circuit.

For many people who didn't live in Haight Ashbury or San Francisco in those halcyon days, Jefferson Airplane, and their antecedents, probably came closest to epitomising all that was great about that free-flowing West Coast sound.

"The magic of the night-time had fallen away to the reality of the morning. It was a pretty bedraggled bunch out there, including the guys on stage." ~ Jack Casady

DAY THREE
SUNDAY 17 AUGUST 1969

The third day, like the second day of Woodstock rolled into the next day. Given the fact that it ran over to Monday, and that many people were exhausted from what had gone before, the crowd started to thin out on Sunday evening. There was a deluge of rain on Sunday afternoon, which is what started the exodus. As *Life* magazine said, "Two rain storms in three days – not a bad average for the Catskills."

2:00pm JOE COCKER

Then the rains came...

6:30pm COUNTRY JOE & THE FISH

8:00pm TEN YEARS AFTER

10:00pm THE BAND

12:00pm JOHNNY WINTER

1:30am BLOOD, SWEAT & TEARS

3:00am CROSBY, STILLS, NASH & YOUNG

6:00am THE PAUL BUTTERFIELD BLUES BAND

7:30am SHA NA NA

9:00am JIMI HENDRIX

JOE COCKER

Page 24—MELODY MAKER, November 16, 1968

MIDDLE EARTH

presents at the

ROUNDHOUSE

CHALK FARM   229 1438

Friday, November 15th

THE WHO ☉ JOE COCKER

SMALL FACES

CRAZY WORLD OF

ARTHUR BROWN

MINDBENDERS   •   YES

JEFF DEXTER   •   LIGHTS   •   SOUNDS

Saturday, November 16th   10.30-Dawn

CRAZY WORLD OF

THE WHO ☉ ARTHUR BROWN

SMALL FACES

MINDBENDERS   •   TEA & SYMPHONY

JEFF DEXTER   •   LIGHTS   •   EVENTS

Advance tickets each night: Members 21/-, Guests 31/-,
from Simon Stable Underground Records
297 Portobello Road; Town Records, King's Road

Membership now only 5/-

Free membership for students

JOHN ROBERT COCKER had not long turned twenty-five when he appeared at Woodstock, but he was no overnight sensation. He had left school in Sheffield, England and become a gas-fitter by day while playing drums and harmonica in his brother's skiffle group, The Cavaliers. By 1963 they had become Vance Arnold and The Avengers with Joe Cocker temporarily changing his name. In 1964 they landed a contract with Decca, but it was really just Cocker they wanted and he recorded a solo version of Lennon and McCartney's 'I'll Cry Instead'; it failed to chart.

He then spent a year touring army bases in France as Joe Cocker's Big Blues but returned, disillusioned, to Sheffield. Back to being a gas fitter he formed The Grease Band in 1965 and for a year they played 'soul covers' in the North of England's pubs and clubs. Their first recording, 'Saved,' was given away with a Sheffield University magazine on a free flexi-disc, before a demo of their self penned 'Marjorine' found it's way to Denny Cordell; he produced 'Whiter Shade of Pale' for Procul Harum. At the session to

"When Cocker and his partner Chris Stainton arrived in London they were wide-eyed and behaved as though they were in a world of fantasy." ~ Tony Visconti, who worked with Denny Cordell on Joe's early singles

**SUNDAY
17 AUGUST**

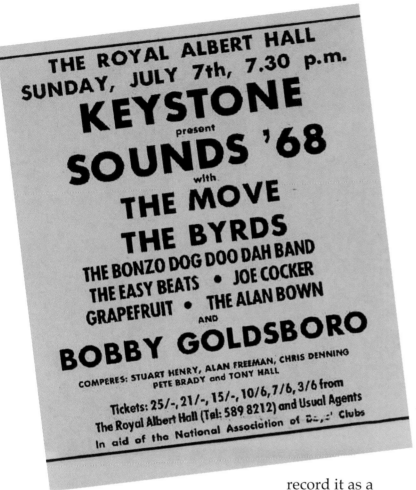

Joe Cocker (1968)

featured Jimmy Page and Stevie Winwood. It set the pattern for much of his later work with its unique interpretations of other people's songs. He covered Dylan, Dave Mason's 'Feelin' Alright' (which dropped out of the *Billboard* chart the week before Joe played Woodstock having peaked at No. 69) and Pete Dello's glorious 'Do I Still Figure in Your Life?' Shortly before Woodstock, The Grease Band had some significant changes in personnel with Stainton switching to keyboards and Alan Spenner (bass) and Bruce Rowlands (drums) completing the line-up.

> ## "I was the only Irish musician to play there, but it was never a big deal. I've seen gigs a lot more chaotic than Woodstock."
> ~ Henry McCullough

record it as a single the only Grease Band member to play was bassist Chris Stainton; he was joined by Jimmy Page and Albert Lee on guitars and Clem Cattini on drums. 'Marjorine' spent a week on the U.K. charts, but the follow-up, an idiosyncratic cover of The Beatles' 'With A Little Help from My Friends,' went to No. 1 in the U.K.; it reached No. 68 in America at the very end of 1968. Henry McCullough had joined the band to play guitar by the time of Cocker's debut album, which also

PERFORMANCE
Some people have suggested that Joe Cocker's performance shaped Woodstock. Maybe it did, but more likely they are talking about how

---

60-MINUTE SET

SET LIST
Delta Lady
Something's Coming On
Do I Still Figure In Your Life
Feelin' Alright
40,000 Headmen
Dear Landlord
Just Like A Woman
I Don't Need No Doctor
I Shall Be Released
Let's Go Get Stoned
With A Little Help From My Friends

THE BAND
Joe Cocker - Vocals
Henry McCullough - Rhythm guitar, Backing Vocals
Alan Spenner - Bass, Backing Vocals
Chris Stainton - Keyboard
Bruce Rowlands - Drums
Bobby Torres - Congas

Joe Cocker, backed by Henry McCullough and Alan Spenner, at Woodstock, Sunday 17 August 1969

"Chris Stainton told me (later) that all the guys in the band had dropped acid, and I was the only guy that hadn't." ~ Joe Cocker

Cocker was captured on film and became an essential ingredient in the movie. 'With A Little Help From My Friends' was Joe's encore and the intensity of his performance amazed everyone when they watched the film.

Most of Joe's set was covers of other artists' songs and every one was a great song that Joe was able to enhance with his inimitable style. Joe's career has always been defined by his choice of cover songs and it's a testament to his 'ears' that he instinctively knew what worked for him.

THE WOODSTOCK EFFECT

Within a couple of weeks of Woodstock Joe Cocker was in Los Angeles working on a new album with Leon Russell. Cocker's version of Russell's 'Delta Lady' made No. 10 in the U.K. and No. 69 in the U.S.A. at the end of the decade; it was also his last record with The Grease Band. Cocker's chart breakthrough in the U.S. was his version of another Lennon and McCartney song – 'She Came In Through The Bathroom Window' in early 1970.

Cocker then decided, with Russell and Cordell's help, to put together 21 musicians who became known as Mad Dogs & Englishmen. They included Carl Radle (bass), Bobby Keys (sax), Jim Keltner (drums) and Don Preston (guitar). They toured America in a private aircraft, made a live album and a feature film about the tour. They had a hit in '70 with a cover of The Box Tops' 'The Letter' (U.K. No. 39/U.S. No. 7). Later in the year 'Cry Me A River' made No. 11 in the U.S.A. and the following year 'High Time We Went' was also a hit. Cocker then took temporary shelter from the music business before he was tempted to return to front the Chris Stainton Band; they had a hit in the U.S.A. in late '72 with 'Midnight Rider' and toured the U.K. as the 12-piece. Cocker, though, was in a pretty bad way through drink and drugs, he often could not remember his words, and not surprisingly the band fell apart after the tour. In 1975 Cocker recorded 'You Are So Beautiful,' co-written with Billy Preston, that went top five in the U.S.A. The rest of the 1970s were a pretty fallow time for Cocker but by the 1980s he reinvented himself recording with jazz funk band The Crusaders. Then in 1982 he once again topped the charts, this time in America, in a duet with Jennifer Warnes singing on 'Up Where We Belong,' the love theme from the film *Officer and A Gentleman*.

From the mid 1980s Cocker had a number of hits on both sides of the Atlantic, although none were placed very high in the charts. In 1994 he played the Woodstock '94 Festival, one of the few survivors from the first time around. Today he lives in Colorado, tours occasionally and will always be a legend for his performance at Woodstock.

Mad Dogs & Englishmen
(1969)

COUNTRY JOE & THE FISH

IN 1965, Barry 'The Fish' Melton began his career as a guitarist and singer while working with 'Country Joe' McDonald as a duo playing folk and jug band music. The Fish took his nickname from Mao Zedong's maxim that the true revolutionary "moves through the peasantry as the fish does through water." Their early gigs were strongly against the war in Vietnam; it was a stance that the band maintained throughout its unfolding existence.

The addition of drummer Gary 'Chicken' Hirsch, David Cohen on keyboards and Doug Metzner playing bass, created music that was at the forefront of San Francisco's emerging sound. Their debut album *Electric*

Electric Music For The Mind And Body (1967)

Music For The Mind and Body that came out in January 1967, was one of the earliest examples of psychedelic rock and San Francisco radio stations KSAN and KMPX did much to champion the band's work. From local favorites they soon established a national reputation as their debut made No. 39 on the *Billboard* album chart; it was quickly followed in by two more albums, *I-Feel-Like-I'm-Fixin-To-Die* in May 1967 and *Together* in 1968. Their third album almost broke into the *Billboard* Top 20 albums, getting to No. 23 in the late summer of 1968. Having appeared at the Monterey Pop Festival in 1967 it was almost inconceivable that Woodstock, with its strong anti-war position and the mood of the movement, could take place with out Country Joe & The Fish; even though the rest of the band's line-up had changed since its early days.

I-Feel-Like-I'm-Fixing-To-Die (1967)

PERFORMANCE

After the three-hour rain and thunderstorm, Country Joe McDonald took the stage for the second time at

SUNDAY 17 AUGUST

"It made me infamous and famous at the same time. To this day it's still a millstone." ~ Country Joe McDonald's take on his notorious 'Fish Cheer'

"I thought, oh my God, here's all these people and the band's never going to get to play." ~ Barry 'The Fish' Melton

45-MINUTE SET

SET LIST
Rock And Soul Music
Thing Called Love
Barry's Caviar Dream
Not So Sweet Martha Lorraine
Love Machine
The 'Fish' Cheer
I-Feel-Like-I'm-Fixin'-To-Die Rag

There were another half dozen songs, at least, in their set but they have gone unrecorded. Around this time they were regularly featuring 'Flying High' and 'Here I Go Again' so it seems likely that they were in the set.

THE BAND
Country Joe McDonald - Guitar, Vocals
Barry 'The Fish' Melton - Guitar, Vocals
Greg 'Duke' Dewey - Drums
Mark Kapner - Keyboards, Organ
Doug Metzner - Bass

Woodstock, but this time it was in his regular guise as the front man for The Fish. Barry Melton was worried that the band wouldn't get to appear at all if the rain kept up. He went on stage and started up the "no rain, no rain" chant in an effort to stop the deluge and to therefore save his big moment. By the time the band played after the rain stopped, he had been on stage, along with Greg 'Duke' Dewey, the band's drummer, for close to three hours leading the chant.

Some of the band's set goes unrecorded, either on tape or in a fan's notebook (did anyone keep one?).

THE WOODSTOCK EFFECT

After releasing the *CJ Fish* album in 1970, Country Joe effectively went solo recording an album of folk songs written by Woody Guthrie; a year later he recorded an electric album. Never wavering from his anti-war position, he incurred President Nixon's wrath in the process. Barry Melton kept the band together for a while but later started working under his own name. Peter Albin and David Getz from Big Brother & the Holding Company joined him for a while and they appeared together in a band called, appropriately, The Dinosaurs, with John Cippolina from Quicksilver Messenger Service.

Barry had started to study law way back in the Sixties and by 1982 he was admitted to practice law in the State of California; much of his work since that time has been as a Public Defender.

CJ Fish (1970)

TEN YEARS AFTER

BEFORE THEIR appearance at Woodstock, Ten Years After were just another British blues band with jazz overtones. After the festival the band, and Alvin Lee their guitarist in particular, were elevated to superstar status. And all this without the need for anyone to die!

"The Woodstock film was partially responsible for some of the misconceptions about the group. The film had a lot of people convinced that we were 'I'm Going Home' and that old rock syndrome that went with it but it was just one facet of the band." ~ Alvin Lee

Ten Years After were another band who were no overnight sensation, having started out in the Nottinghamshire area in 1960 as Ivan Jay and the Jaycats; to begin with they were just another beat band. It was just Alvin and Leo Lyons of the Woodstock line up in the original band with Ric Lee joining in 1965 (Ric was no relation to Alvin, who's real name was the much-less-glamourous-sounding

Graham Barnes); Chick Churchill joined a year later, by which time the band had moved to London to make it big. After several more name changes they finally settled on Ten Years After in 1966; Alvin Lee idolized Elvis Presley and this was ten years after 1956, Elvis' *annus mirabilis*.

Their big break came in 1967 when they played the National Jazz & Blues Festival held at Windsor Racecourse to the west of London. This led to the band signing for Deram Records and releasing their self-titled debut album in October of that year.

Among the tracks was an excellent cover of Al Kooper's 'I Can't Keep from Crying Sometimes.' In 1968 they released *Undead*, a live album that showcased the band's great stage show; it made the UK charts in the fall of 1968. It featured 'I'm Going

Home,' which the band played so effectively at Woodstock; it was the birth of Alvin Lee – guitar god. They followed *Undead* with their second studio album, *Stonehenge*, in February 1969, which made the Top 10 of the U.K. album charts. By the time they got to

Ten Years After (1967)

"I've got a jumble of memories. The most vivid is the journey in, because we could only get within about ten miles of the site and no nearer, the roads were all jammed. So we bundled into an army helicopter with an open side and I had a safety harness on. I was dangling out of the helicopter over half-a-million people."
~ Alvin Lee

Woodstock, Ten Years After were little known in America and while they were gaining a growing body of fans in Britain they were far from superstars; the festival was their big break.

PERFORMANCE
The humidity-ravaged instruments was just one of the problems for the band. The sound recording worked sporadically and the film crew were only able to film Ten Years After's last song. At over 12 minutes long 'I'm Going Home' confirmed Ten Years After as a powerhouse band and elevated Alvin Lee to guitar's top table from the moment the film was released. As a tribute to what Alvin loved so much it featured 'Blue Suede Shoes,' 'Whole Lotta Shakin' Goin' On' and John Lee Hooker's 'Boom Boom' within this repetitive riff-based rock'n'roll song.

60-MINUTE SET

SET LIST
Waiting*
The Hobbit*
Spoonful
Good Morning Little Schoolgirl
I Can't Keep From Crying Sometimes
I May Be Wrong, But I Won't Be Wrong
Always
I'm Going Home
* The first two songs on the list are probable songs...

THE BAND
Alvin Lee - Guitar, Vocals
Chick Churchill - Organ
Leo Lyons - Bass
Ric Lee - Drums

"There was a lot of humidity which played havoc with the guitar strings. I remember starting 'Good Morning Little Schoolgirl' four times. It's weird starting a number four times in front of 500,000 people." ~ Ric Lee

Ten Years After: Leo Lyons and Alvin Lee, 1975

"'You can't go on now you might get electrocuted' – there was still some rain – and I just said, 'Oh come on, if I get electrocuted at Woodstock we'll sell lots of records.'" ~ Alvin Lee

But all is not as it seems with the recording. The sound problems meant that Ric Lee's drums went unrecorded for the most part and the bits that were audible were of poor quality. It required a studio overdub, but not from Ric himself. Mountain's roadie and future drummer, Canadian Corky Laing, did them in the studio; Corky replaced Mountain's drummer very soon after Woodstock.

THE WOODSTOCK EFFECT

Ten Years After were another band for whom Woodstock changed their status around the world and particularly in America. Their first post-festival album was *Ssssh*, which came out in early September 1969, becoming their biggest hit to date, making No. 20 in the U.S.A. and going Top 5 in Britain staying on the charts for the next five months. Its centerpiece was 'Good Morning Little School Girl,' Sonny Boy Williamson's un-PC blues classic. They

Ssssh (1969)

had recorded it shortly before leaving for Woodstock and it was one of the standout songs in their festival set. In May 1970 they released *Cricklewood Green* and from this album came their only single to chart in Britain and their first chart hit in America: 'Love Like a Man' made No. 98 on the *Billboard* chart, but made the Top 10 in Britain. The band had one more big album in Britain when *Watt* made No. 5 in 1971 and it also reached No. 21 in the U.S.A. Their next album, A *Space In Time* was a far bigger hit in America but it was the beginnings of a slow decline in the band's fortunes; their last success on the charts was a live album in 1973. After the release of their 1974 album, *Positive Vibrations,* the band broke up. They did reunite briefly in the 1980s but without any real success. Alvin Lee continues to release albums under his own name, the most recent being *Saguitar* in September 2007.

Saguitar (2007)

THE BAND

WOODSTOCK WAS VERY MUCH a hometown gig for The Band; the band that had been a band for almost a decade before they took the stage at Woodstock. Robertson, Hudson, Manuel and Danko are all Canadians, with Helm their token American. They had come together initially as rockabilly singer Ronnie Hawkins' backing band – they were known back then as The Hawks. By 1964 they had left Hawkins and in 1965 they were recruited by Bob Dylan to back him on an American tour, which was followed by a world tour the following year; during 1967 they backed Dylan on what have become known as *The*

Basement Tapes. It was during a Dylan gig in Manchester, England in May 1966 someone in the audience dared to call His Bobness "Judas" for playing electric music with The Band.

Music From Big Pink (1968)

Between their Dylan world tour, which Helm didn't appear on, and the recording of *The Basement Tapes* in the summer of 1967, The Band played minor gigs and even backed the bizarre Tiny Tim in the film *You Are What You Eat*. Dylan had a motorcycle accident in July 1966, and it was only after he recovered that he invited The Band to come to Woodstock to work with him on new material.

"Those songs are part of the American heritage now."
~ Ralph Gleason, reviewing The Band at Winterland in May 1969

In early 1968, having been signed by Capitol Records, they started work on their own album, but to begin with they had no definite name. It was only when test pressings of their album arrived with the moniker 'The Band' on them that they began using it – with some reservations. When *Music from Big Pink* was released in July it received instant critical

From The States..
featuring
Ronnie Hawkins **The Band**
(Now Dylan's backing group)
Who Do You Love b/w **Bo Diddley** RO512

AND HIS LP

RONNIE HAWKINS
ARKANSAS ROCK PILE
featuring THE BAND

...The greatest rock release in years...12 original tracks at the give away price of only 19/11...

"ARKANSAS ROCK PILE" A ROULETTE Record Mono Only **RCP1003**

Robbie Robertson and Levon Helm at Woodstock, 17 August 1969

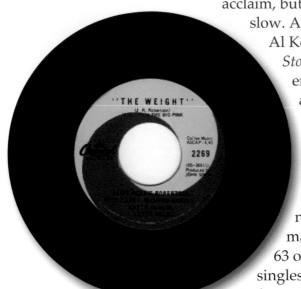

First pressings of 'The Weight' are credited to Jaime Robbie Robertson, Rick Danko, Richard Manuel, Garth Hudson and Levon Helm. They were, at this point, a band with no name.

acclaim, but initially sales were slow. After a rave review by Al Kooper in *Rolling Stone* sales increased, it entered the U.S. album chart in October climbing to No. 30. The Band had also released a single, 'The Weight,' and while sales were not great it did manage to make No. 63 on the *Billboard* singles chart and got good airplay on the alternative stations. The album's title is derived from the house that they rented in West Saugerties, close to Woodstock; it was used to rehearse the music that was later recorded in Los Angeles and New York.

"This album was recorded in approximately two weeks. There are people who will work their lives away in vain and not touch it." ~ Al Kooper reviews *Music From Big Pink* in *Rolling Stone*

'The Weight' was used in the film *Easy Rider* which came out a month before Woodstock, so The Band's collateral was peaking following extensive touring in support of their album. Interestingly, when the *Easy Rider* soundtrack album came out in early August 'The Weight' was performed by an unknown Los Angeles rock band called Smith, due to contractual issues with using The Band's version. It did Smith's career no good and perversely did The Band no harm.

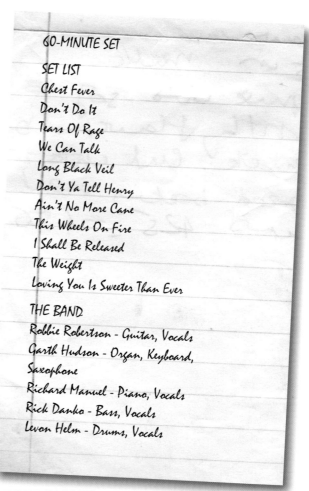

60-MINUTE SET

SET LIST
Chest Fever
Don't Do It
Tears Of Rage
We Can Talk
Long Black Veil
Don't Ya Tell Henry
Ain't No More Cane
This Wheels On Fire
I Shall Be Released
The Weight
Loving You Is Sweeter Than Ever

THE BAND
Robbie Robertson - Guitar, Vocals
Garth Hudson - Organ, Keyboard, Saxophone
Richard Manuel - Piano, Vocals
Rick Danko - Bass, Vocals
Levon Helm - Drums, Vocals

PERFORMANCE

Introduced onto the stage by Chip Monck, The Band launched their set with Garth Hudson's brilliant opening organ refrain from 'Chest Fever' taken from their *Music From Big Pink* album. The majority of the set came from the album; it was at the time their only recording as a group. 'Tears of Rage,' 'Ain't No More

Cane' and 'Don't Ya Tell Henry' were all on the Basement Tapes as was 'This Wheel's On Fire,' which they covered on *Music from Big Pink*.

"I had mixed feelings about it, because at the festival we were the only people that actually lived at Woodstock." ~ Robbie Robertson

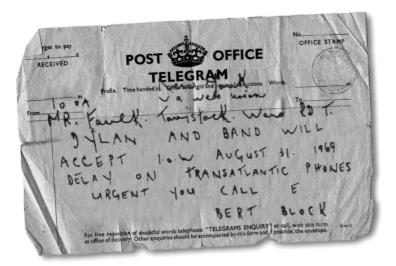

THE WOODSTOCK EFFECT

At the end of August 1969 The Band were in the UK appearing at the Isle of Wight Festival. They

The Band   (1969)

performed on their own, largely the same songs as the ones they did at Woodstock, as well as appearing with Bob Dylan to perform a set that was none too well received by the British public. Upon their return from the UK The Band released their

follow-up to *Music from Big Pink*. Cunningly entitled *The Band* it was a step farther along the rustic road that had begun with their debut. Stylistically it was in the same territory as Dylan's *John Wesley Harding* and

Richard Manuel at Woodstock, 17 August 1969

Stage Fright (1970)

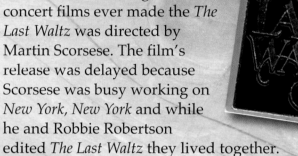

The Byrds' *Sweethearts of the Rodeo*. 'Up on Cripple Creek,' the album's lead-off single release almost made the *Billboard* Top 20 (No. 25) and helped propel the album to No. 9 on the U.S. chart.

Having joined Janis Joplin, The Grateful Dead and others on the 'Festival Express' fiasco The Band set about recoding their third album. *Stage Fright* turned out to be a pale shadow of their earlier efforts. Despite that, or maybe because of that, it did manage to make No. 5 on the U.S. charts, although it sold in fewer numbers than *The Band*. It also marked the long slow beginning of the end of The Band; the cracks in their once tight on- and off-stage harmony were showing. 1971's *Cahoots* failed to make the Top 20, although the live album *Rock of Ages* briefly stemmed the tide (No. 6 in 1972) by the time 1973's covers album, *Moondog Matinee*, came out it could only make No. 28.

In 1974 they worked again with Dylan recording *Planet Waves*, touring with him and appearing on the live album *Before The Flood*. In 1975 The Band released their first album of new material since 1971. *Northern Lights-Southern Cross* was a commercial failure – the critics disagreed. By 1976, wearied of it all, The Band decided to call it a day with a huge concert at San Francisco's Winterland in November – Thanksgiving Day. *The Last Waltz* as it was dubbed, did well as an album and the much later DVD release has also proved popular, featuring as it does, Dylan, Muddy

The Last Waltz (1978)

Waters, Eric Clapton, Neil Young and Neil Diamond among a cast of music's great and good. Hailed as one of the greatest concert films ever made the *The Last Waltz* was directed by Martin Scorsese. The film's release was delayed because Scorsese was busy working on *New York, New York* and while he and Robbie Robertson edited *The Last Waltz* they lived together.

The Band did reunite, but minus Robbie Robertson with whom the others had fallen out in 1983; but tragically Richard Manuel committed suicide in 1985. He had suffered from alcoholism for many years. The Band continued with various substitute pianists. Rick Danko died in his sleep aged 56 in 1999. When the Band received a Grammy lifetime achievement award in 2008 Helm didn't attend, the rift with Robertson still appeared to be too deep.

JOHNNY WINTER

EVEN BEFORE HIS WOODSTOCK appearance Johnny Winter's stock was high among the world's great guitar players, men who know a fellow traveler when they hear one. In January and February of 1969, Winter was playing sell-out shows at the Fillmore East in New York earning around $7,500 a night; Columbia Records had signed him with a very large advance. The man they called the Albino Elvis Presley was very definitely THE next big thing.

> ## "Playing lounges, bars, mostly in the South. Whatever was happening musically at the time, we played it. Soul, whatever the drunks wanted to hear."
> ~ Johnny Winter

The twenty-five-year-old John Dawson Winter III from Beaumont was a blues guitarist with a prodigious talent, one that had been honed from playing the bars and clubs of his native Texas; he earned $50 in a good week. Having originally played in a band called It and Them with his brother Edgar, another albino, they changed their name to Johnny Winter and The Black Plague before Winter formed his own group with bassist Tommy Shannon and John Turner on drums. Their first album was made sometime in 1968 for the Imperial label; it failed to get a release until after he signed to Columbia. Called *The Progressive Blues Experiment* it pretty much did

LIVE! AT THE
FAIRFIELD, CROYDON
SUNDAY, APRIL 19th
at 6 p.m. and 8.45 p.m.
JOHN & TONY SMITH PRESENT

TAJ MAHAL AND **JOHNNY WINTERS**

IN CONCERT
Seats: 20/-, 17/-, 15/-, 13/-, 10/-
Box Office Tel.: 688 9291

what it said on the cover and is considered by many Winter aficionados to be one of his best albums.

Winter's Columbia debut came out in May 1969 to muted acclaim – sometimes the hype backfires – but some healthy sales took it to just outside the Top 20 of the U.S. album charts just before Woodstock. The album also features brother Edgar along with blues legends Willie Dixon and Walter Horton. A little over a month before Woodstock The Rolling Stones opened their Hyde Park free concert

The Progressive Blues Experiment (1969)

Johnny Winter at Woodstock, 17 August 1969

with Winter's 'I'm Hers And I'm Yours,' the first track on side one of his Columbia debut.

"I think it was Keith who came up with the idea of doing Johnny Winter's 'I'm Hers And I'm Yours,' but to be honest we didn't do a very good job with it. We hardly had any time to rehearse it."
~ Bill Wyman

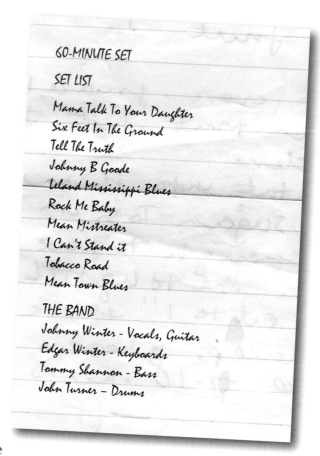

60-MINUTE SET

SET LIST

Mama Talk To Your Daughter
Six Feet In The Ground
Tell The Truth
Johnny B Goode
Leland Mississippi Blues
Rock Me Baby
Mean Mistreater
I Can't Stand it
Tobacco Road
Mean Town Blues

THE BAND

Johnny Winter - Vocals, Guitar
Edgar Winter - Keyboards
Tommy Shannon - Bass
John Turner - Drums

PERFORMANCE
'Mean Town Blues,' the band's encore, was featured in the film *The Woodstock Diaries* and is the only song in Johnny Winter's set to have come from his *Progressive Blues Experiment* album that came out a couple of months before Woodstock. In the main his material came from his first Columbia album, with 'Johnny B. Goode' the only cut from the album he was to record just after his festival appearance. Edgar joined his brother on stage for 'I Can't Stand It' and 'Tobacco Road.'

THE WOODSTOCK EFFECT

In the immediate aftermath of Woodstock Johnny Winter's band, along with Edgar, were back in the studio to record *Second Winter*, their Columbia follow-up. It was a much better album than the first

Second Winter (1969)

one and helped to justify some of the hype that surrounded their signing, but it did nothing to assuage the Columbia executives that had paid what the music press was saying was one of the "biggest new artist's advances in their history" – in reality $600,000 over five years. *Second Winter* failed to chart in America, but did just make the Top 75 in Britain, which in some ways is inexplicable because it was a fine album of original blues and great covers. It was also unique in being a 3-sided album; one side of the second LP was left blank (very Seventies!).

The lack of success of *Second Winter* encouraged Winter to change musical tack for his 1970 album, *Johnny Winter And*. The 'And' were Rick Derringer, Randy Jo Hobbs and Randy Zehringer. Drummer Randy Z was Rick's brother, Rick's surname being

"Johnny always said he was great. He just wanted other people to know it too." ~ Edgar Winter, February 1969

Johnny Winter And (1970)

Still Alive And Well (1973)

Zehringer, and along with bass-playing Hobbs they had made up most of Sixties band The McCoys, whose biggest hit 'Hang On Sloopy' went to No. 1 on the *Billboard* chart in 1965. Derringer was another fine guitarist and a great foil for Winter's playing on their first album together – a great psychedelic, blues, rock affair. While it charted in Britain it did badly in America, but it was as a live band that they really came good. Their show, mixing blues with rock'n'roll standards along with Winter's originals was as exciting as anything on the tour circuit in 1970 and '71. Their stage show was in part captured on *Johnny Winter And – Live* but like all great live albums there's still that feeling that it would have been better to have been there. For those that did manage to catch the twin lead guitar interplay between Winter and Derringer live on stage it's a poignant, yet rocking, reminder of what might have been had they been together at the time of Woodstock.

Johnny Winter had a heroin problem from early on in his career and he temporarily retired from the scene for about a year to cleanse himself, and when he returned he made an album in 1973 appropriately entitled *Still Alive and Well*. Six more albums followed in the Seventies and since then another 10 have appeared. Nothing has matched his early success but Johnny Winter remains a stellar blues guitarist, touring and playing old-style blues as well as the high-energy material from his heyday – including a scorching cover of Dylan's 'Highway 61 Revisited' which had originally appeared on *Second Winter*.

BLOOD, SWEAT & TEARS

Child Is Father To The Man
(1968)

FORMED IN 1967 out of the ashes of The Blues Project, who had played Monterey in 1967, by Al Kooper and guitarist Steve Katz, Blood, Sweat & Tears were named by Kooper after cutting his hand and covering his organ with blood at a gig, not after a Johnny Cash album as it states all over the web. They signed to Columbia Records and the line-up was completed by Fred Lipsius, Randy Brecker (trumpet), Jerry Weiss (trumpet), Dick Halligan, Jim Fielder and Bobby Colomby. Their first album was recorded in November and December and was intriguingly entitled *Child is Father to the Man* – a reference to a poem by Gerad Manley Hopkins. Released in February 1968 it was immediately loved by the critics and barely noticed by most of the public, only creeping into the album chart at No. 47; it was later nominated for a Grammy, and in 2003 would make the top 300 in the *Rolling Stone* Top 500 albums of all time – it really is that good. It benefited from the superbly creative mind of Al Kooper and contains some of the most inventive rock of the time. Soon after the album came out Brecker and Weiss were replaced by Lew Soloff and Chuck Winfield; trombonist Jerry Hyman was also added. Most importantly Kooper left the band.

"I had cut my hand playing and in a state of bliss induced by my compatriots' sound had not felt a thing. What a great album cover, I thought. No, what a great name for a band." ~ Al Kooper

Kooper's departure created a creative hole and a vocal vacancy, which was filled by Canadian, but British born, David Clayton-Thomas and this completed the line-up that was to appear at Woodstock a year later. They finished their self-titled *Blood, Sweat & Tears* album in October 1968 and it came out two months later. It's been called more obviously pop than rock, yet it was at the time a far more experimental album, fusing jazz with classical music (Satie's *Trois Gymnopédies*), blues and soul. It benefited from David Clayton-Thomas' singing and some ambitious arrangements. It made the American album charts in January 1969 and stayed at No. 1 from late in March for seven weeks; it was also nominated for a Grammy. 'You've Made Me So Very Happy' reached No. 2 as did the follow-up, 'Spinning Wheel' (just before Woodstock) and 'And When I Die.' The band was one of the hottest acts to be booked to play the festival, having also appeared at several others over the course of the summer.

**MONDAY
18 AUGUST**

"He was staggering… a powerfully built singer who exuded an enormous earthy confidence. He jumped right out at you. A perfect combination of fire and emotion to go with the band's somewhat cerebral appeal." ~ Clive Davis on David Clayton-Thomas

PERFORMANCE

Not their finest hour, according to saxophonist and pianist Fred Lipsius who claims that David Clayton-Thomas sang out of tune all through their set – apparently a unique occurrence in the history of a truly innovative rock band. However, filmed evidence of Mr. C-T seem to dispel at least some of that myth.

THE WOODSTOCK EFFECT

Having cemented their counterculture credentials by appearing at Woodstock and seemingly overcome the departure of Kooper they then blew it, in the eyes of many of their fans, by doing a tour of Eastern Europe

"Wait, you want us to do a movie – we're going to draw the people to the movie, and you're going to pay us $7,500? No, thank you!" ~ Bobby Colomby recalling why the band failed to appear in the movie

that was sponsored by the U.S. State Department. To make matters worse they even played Las Vegas; from there on in it was pretty much down hill all the way. 'Hi-De-Ho' from their third album made No. 14 on the chart and that was the last time they made the U.S. Top 20 singles chart. The album from which it was taken, *Blood Sweat & Tears 3* did top the album chart for two weeks exactly a year after Woodstock.

Two more albums followed before the end of 1972 and while they did chart they had little to commend them; by the time of *New Blood* in November of 1972 Clayton-Thomas had left to pursue the inevitable solo career. By 1976 the last remaining original member, Bobby Colomby had also left, although he did retain ownership of the band's name. By 1979 they were back together, at least with one original, Clayton-Thomas; by 1981 this incarnation had also ground to a halt. In 1984 Clayton-Thomas was back touring with a new BS&T, having licensed the name from Colomby, and this remained the case for 20 years – with well over 100 musicians passing through the band's ranks. Today there's a Blood, Sweat & Tears, minus Clayton-Thomas, touring the world with just one original member; Steve Katz rejoined the band in 2008.

Blood, Sweat & Tears 3
(1970)

45-MINUTE SET

SET LIST
Just One Smile
More And More
All In A Day
I Love You Baby More Than
    You'll Ever Know
You've Made Me So Very Happy
God Bless The Child
Spinning Wheel
I Stand Accused
Something's Coming On
… and others

THE BAND
David Clayton-Thomas – Vocals, Guitar
Bobby Colomby – Drums
Jim Fielder – Bass
Dick Halligan – Keyboards, Trombone, Flute
Jerry Hyman – Trombone
Steve Katz – Guitar, Harmonica, Vocals
Fred Lipsius – Alto sax, Piano
Lew Soloff – Trumpet, Flugelhorn
Chuck Winfield – Trumpet, Flugelhorn

Blood, Sweat & Tears on stage at the Longhorn Jazz Festival, Dallas, 18 July 1969.
Left to right: Steve Katz, Jim Fielder, David Clayton-Thomas, Jerry Hyman, Chuck Winfield and Lew Soloff

CROSBY, STILLS, NASH & YOUNG

TAKE A HOLLIE, A BYRD and two Buffalo Springfields, not the steamrollers made by the company of that name, but Stephen Stills and Neil Young, and you have Crosby, Stills, Nash & Young. Ex-Byrd David Crosby and Englishman Graham Nash completed what was, in late-Sixties parlance – a supergroup. They were not the first, that was arguably Blind Faith, but they've been one of the best and one of the longest-enduring musical relationships of the rock era and Woodstock was their second-ever gig together

"You are leaving fame, fortune and all these hits? Are you crazy?"
~ The Hollies collectively to Graham Nash

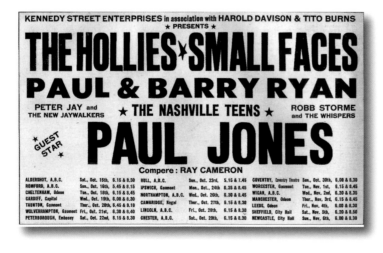

Dallas Taylor, Stephen Stills, David Crosby, Bruce Palmer, Neil Young and Graham Nash, July 1969

Graham Nash and David Crosby at Woodstock, 18 August 1969

When Graham Nash had his first hit record with The Hollies in June 1963 he could scarcely have imagined what would follow; The 21-year-old from Manchester, England could not have predicted that six years later he would be standing on stage at a festival at 3:00am about to entertain those among the crowd, of how ever many hundred thousand, were still awake. Around the same time as The Hollies' first hit, the slightly younger David Van Cortlandt Crosby was making his first record as a folk singer. Two years later, as a member of The Byrds, he was recording his first hit under the watchful eye of Terry Melcher, the son of an American icon – Doris Day. Meanwhile Stephen Stills was dropping out of the University of Florida and heading north, eventually joining the Au Go Go Singers and recording for the first time in 1964. By early 1966 Stills had moved to

and they were joined by Nash; they found their voices just clicked as they performed 'You Don't Have To Cry.'

Crosby, Stills & Nash, the album, came out at the end of May 1969 and was an instant critical and commercial success. It entered the charts in July

Crosby, Stills & Nash (1969)

and eventually peaked at No. 6, helped by the single 'Marrakesh Express'; although it only reached No. 28 on the *Billboard* chart it received a lot of plays on FM radio. This album was a marker for many of their contemporaries, proving to be one of those albums that sounds as fresh today as it did forty years ago.

"A unit with three arms and we can wander out on any one of the arms." ~ Graham Nash describing Crosby, Stills & Nash in May 1969

California, where he met Neil Young and together with Stills' old friend Richie Furay they formed Buffalo Springfield. Neil Young was born in Canada and is the youngest of the four members of CSNY; his first studio sessions were in late 1965 with future Motown funkster Rick James.

After Crosby was evicted from The Byrds, in part over their refusal to record a song of his about a ménage-a-trois, he met Stephen Stills; it was early 1968 and Buffalo Springfield had recently disintegrated. The two men found they shared a musical symbiosis. Nash had first met Crosby when The Byrds toured Britain and renewed their friendship when he went to California after he left The Hollies in late 1968. At a party at Mama Cass's house in February 1969, Stills and Crosby got up to sing a song written by the ex-Buffalo Springfielder

The big problem for the trio was that they needed to tour, and while Dallas Taylor played drums on the album it was the gifted Stills that played most of the other instruments. They decided they needed an additional musician – enter Neil Young who, despite some reservations from Stills, joined in July 1969. He had just started his own band but a contract was worked out enabling him to do both. On August 16 Crosby, Stills, Nash & Young played their first-ever gig together at the Auditorium Theatre in Chicago. Two days later they were at Woodstock.

PERFORMANCE
At 3:00am it was difficult for any artist to be at their best but there's no doubt that Crosby, Stills, Nash & Young were one of the standout performances of the festival. So excited were they by the sound they made

"This is the second time we've ever played in front of people, man. We're scared sh*tless!" ~ Stephen Stills

60 MINUTE SET

ACOUSTIC SET LIST
Suite: Judy Blue Eyes
Blackbird
Helplessly Hoping
Guinevere
Marrakesh Express
4 + 20
Mr. Soul
I'm Wonderin'
You Don't Have To Cry

ELECTRIC SET LIST
Pre Road Downs
Long Time Gone
Bluebird Revisited
Sea Of Madness
Wooden Ships
Find The Cost Of Freedom
49 Bye-Byes

THE BAND
David Crosby - Guitar, Vocals
Stephen Stills - Guitar, Vocals
Graham Nash - Guitar, Vocals
Neil Young - Guitar, Vocals, Organ
Greg Reeves - Bass
Dallas Taylor - Drums

"They had the crowd all the way." ~ Greil Marcus reviewing their set for Rolling Stone

that at one point David Crosby almost fell off the stage. They started out as they would for the next two years of the initial existence as a band by performing their acoustic music and, like their debut album, their set opened with Steve Stills song of losing, written about his former love, singer Judy Collins. They even threw in a cover of The Beatles' song 'Blackbird' and an old Buffalo Springfield classic, 'Mr Soul,' in the 'wooden music' part of their set. It wasn't all impeccable – they fluffed the opening of 'Helplessly Hoping,' Stills asking Nash if he had a 'chicken bone' stuck in his throat.

By the time they went electric with Stills switching to organ to urge the band on through 'Long Time Gone' they were really cooking. Their set climaxed with 'Wooden Ships,' the song written with Jefferson Airplane's Paul Kantner, before they encored with the beautiful 'Find The Cost of Freedom' and '49 Bye-Byes,' their closer from their debut album.

THE WOODSTOCK EFFECT

From Woodstock the band hit the road playing Los Angeles, New York, the ill-fated Altamont Festival and cities across America. They also went into the studio to record their follow-up album. *Déjà Vu* came out in March and totally eclipsed their debut, climbing to No.

Déjà Vu   (1970)

1 in the U.S. and No. 5 in the U.K., where it stayed on the album chart for over a year. Young's voice and songwriting added another dimension to the band, but it was the inclusion of Joni Mitchell's 'Woodstock' that helped the album's sales. The band's version of Joni's song came out as a single in March 1970 and just failed to reach the *Billboard* Top 10.

Off the back of Woodstock came Graham Nash's 'Teach Your Children' which went Top 20, while simultaneously the band's rush release of the song 'Ohio,' recorded following the Kent State campus shootings, went to No. 14. The song was the first

many in the public learned of their political motivation, something that's never left the band. However, despite their success the difficulties of maintaining such a loosely formatted group soon manifested themselves and Crosby, Stills, Nash & Young broke up at the end of their 1970 summer tour.

For the next year the individual talents did their own thing. Crosby released his solo tour-de-force, *If I Could Only Remember My Name*. Neil Young brought out *After The Gold Rush*, Stephen Stills his eponymous album and Graham Nash recorded 'Song For Beginners.' Stills won the chart race, peaking at No. 3 propelled by the success of his single 'Love The One Your With.'

To attempt to chronicle the ups and downs and ins and outs of Crosby, Stills, Nash & Young over the next four decades needs a book of its own. Suffice to say they are still touring together following frequent fallouts, David Crosby's fight against multiple addictions, the vagaries of the record business and the changing tastes of the public. Crosby, Stills, Nash & Young are a dynasty that have, between them, arguably played to more people around the world since the Sixties than just about any other band.

"Neil's effect on the band was immediate and very fulfilling. He adds a certain edge to the sound and, of course, he is an incredible musician. We became a better band because of the inclusion of Neil Young." ~ Graham Nash

THE PAUL BUTTERFIELD

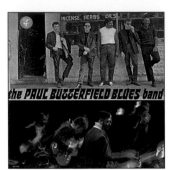

THEY WERE ONCE a great blues band, but by the time a band calling itself The Paul Butterfield Blues Band appeared on stage at Woodstock they were no longer the powerhouse Chicago blues band than many tried to emulate but failed. Butterfield was a white man who really could sing the blues and he was one of the first to gain respect from musicians of whatever color.

The son of a lawyer from the right side of the tracks in Chicago, by 1962 Butterfield was spending his time hanging out with black musicians learning from the likes of Muddy Waters, Junior Wells, Howlin' Wolf and their sidemen. In 1963 The Paul Butterfield Blues Band became the house band at a Chicago club, breaking all the rules by being mixed race. They signed to Elektra Records and set about recording their first album. The self-titled *Paul Butterfield Blues Band* was released in 1965 and almost immediately sold well – unusually so for a blues album. The band was Paul on harmonica and vocals, Mike Bloomfield and Elvin Bishop on guitars, Mark Naftalin (organ), Jerome Arnold (bass) and Sam Lay (drums). It's a masterpiece of the genre and

among the best modern-day blues albums.

By the time of their follow-up, *East–West*, Lay was no longer with the band having accidentally shot himself (Lay recovered to join Muddy Waters' band) and Billy Davenport took his place. This second album was 'of its time' in that it

The Paul Butterfield Blues Band (1965)

had a strong Indian influence, particularly in the raga-based title track. While critically acclaimed it did not sell as well as its predecessor. Soon after Bloomfield left and formed the Electric Flag and went on to have a stellar career working with Al Kooper from Blood, Sweat & Tears. The Butterfield band re-grouped around Elvin Bishop's guitar playing and

BLUES BAND

added a horn section; they played the Monterey Festival with this line-up. Their third album *The Resurrection of Pigboy Crabshaw,* recorded in 1967, highlighted a move to R&B from the blues.

By 1968 Bishop and Naftalin left the band shortly after their fourth album came out. The new guitarist was Buzzy Feiten, and he was in the line-up that recorded *Keep On Moving* which was largely recorded by the band that played Woodstock.

> ## "In all the times I heard him play, man, I never heard him blow a false note. Almost on a nightly basis, he would blow me away, sometimes with a single note, played with just the right feeling."
> ~ Mark Naftalin

East - West   (1966)

PERFORMANCE
Probably the best that can be said about the band's Woodstock performance is they were great musicians stuck in completely the wrong environment to get the recognition they deserved. They were more jazz than rock and had none of the song recognition of a band like Blood, Sweat & Tears. The Butterfield Band works best on 'Drifting Blues,' the old Charles Brown classic; it features some great sax playing from future saxophone legend David Sanborn, Feiten's fabulous guitar playing and some lovely electric piano from Ted Harris. It works best of all because Butterfield blows harmonica better than just about anyone ever has.

THE WOODSTOCK EFFECT
As he didn't feature in the original movie, Butterfield had very little positive effect from his Woodstock appearance and in late 1970 the band broke up, and he went to live in Woodstock putting together a new band he called Better Days that included Maria and Geoff Muldaur. They released a couple of albums, after which Butterfield himself worked as a session musician as well as touring with Rick Danko of The Band and later working with Levon Helm, who had also been in The Band. There were sporadic albums until 1986's *The Legendary Paul Butterfield Rides Again.* It proved to be his swan song as he died from a heart attack in May 1987; years of hard living finally caught up with him.

45-MINUTE SET

SET LIST
- All In A Day
- All My Love Comin' Through To You
- Morning Sunrise
- Drifting Blues
- Born Under A Bad Sign
- Love March
- Everything's Gonna Be Alright

THE BAND
- Paul Butterfield - Harmonica, Vocals
- Buzzy Feiten - Guitar
- Rod Hicks - Bass
- Ted Harris - Keyboards
- Phillip Wilson - Drums
- Steve Madaio - Trumpet
- Keith Johnson - Trumpet
- David Sanborn - Alto saxophone
- Trevor Lawrence - Baritone saxophone
- Gene Dinwiddie - Tenor saxophone

SHA NA NA

FOR SHA NA NA, walking on stage at 7:30am on the Monday morning of the festival to play a set of high-energy classic rock'n'roll as the 'warm-up act' for Jimi Hendrix should have ended in disaster. As it was the twelve-man group of musicians, singers and dancers pulled it off and had a ball doing it. Twenty years later George Leonard, the man whose idea it was to recreate the heady days of ice-cream parlors and Fifties drive-ins into a performing group, and the band's singer, Rob Leonard, recalled what it was like to appear at Woodstock in the Columbia College magazine. "So five months after George had told us in Rob's apartment that he was going to teach us to dance and make us stars, a bunch of Columbia guys who had merely signed up for a King's Crown Activity were staring dumbfounded out the open door of a troop transport helicopter as it flew over miles of hippies, abandoned cars, smashed fences, campfires and wandering day-glo-colored armies looking for water and food and dope."

The group started out at Columbia University as The Kingsmen, an a cappella outfit, but soon after they changed their name because of the other better-known band of the same name. Early in 1969 their agent suggested they call themselves The Put-Ons so George Leonard, who had conceived the idea and choreographed the group, changed their name to Sha Na Na, promising to change it as soon as he thought of something better. Somehow everything clicked into place and bookings flooded in from all over the New York area. Michael Lang had seen them at one of these gigs and come backstage to tell them "You guys have got to be in Woodstock." No-one was quite sure who he was and he nearly got thrown out – none of them had a clue what Woodstock was.

Today, with a far stronger visual element in music thanks to MTV and videos, we have all come to expect that bands dance and sing in an effort to sell their music. Back in 1969 the concept was far less accepted, and certainly the idea of the tie-dye generation accepting such a concept would have seemed pretty far-fetched if you had asked anyway before their appearance. In fact, Sha Na Na were just right for the time and just right for Woodstock. Everyone in the audience knew their songs and, like the very best cover bands, they added an extra ingredient that helped to make it work for them. In the case of Sha Na Na it was a unique blend of music, acting, dancing, singing, performing, choreography and razz-a-matazz – kind of Little Richard meets Busby Berkeley.

"Rock'n'roll has nothing to do with a generation gap anymore. Nowadays, it's really a generation bridge." ~ Sha Na Na vocalist Donny York

PERFORMANCE
Sha Na Na were captured on film and appeared in the movie, so its possible to appreciate just what they were all about. In fact, their stage act was highly polished even this early in their career.

MONDAY
18 AUGUST

218

Keith Moon of The Who joins Sha Na Na on stage at Crystal Palace, London on 3 June 1972

"We did 40 minutes and were paid $300… and the check bounced!"
~ Sha Na Na drummer Jocko Marcellino

THE WOODSTOCK EFFECT

Like Santana and Joe Cocker, Sha Na Na's career had a huge boost from their Woodstock appearance; it was almost as though they kick-started a Fifties nostalgia boom. The TV series *Happy Days* was a direct descendent, the musical *Grease* hit Broadway and the band itself appeared in the movie version in 1978. From 1977 until 1981, the band that had by this time had a number of personnel changes got its own TV series that attracted huge ratings. Their live work never did translate into hit singles; they had just two *Billboard* hits in 1971. There was 'Top Forty' and '(Just Like) Romeo and Juliet' in 1975. Individuals from the original Woodstock band pursued a whole variety of paths. Rob Leonard became a professor of linguistics; Henry Gross had a solo hit with a lovely song called 'Shannon' in 1976 (it was about his dog). Al Cooper taught religious studies, becoming the group's second professor. Elliot Cahn later managed Green Day, while Joe Witkin is a physician and Scott Powell a surgeon. Frederick Greene became a lawyer, worked for Columbia Pictures and is the band's third professor.

Sha Na Na   (1971)

30-MINUTE SET

SET LIST
'Na Na Theme'
'Yakety Yak'
'Teen Angel'
'Jailhouse Rock'
'Wipe Out'
'(Who Wrote) The Book of Love'
'Duke Of Earl'
'At the Hop'
'Na Na Theme'

The Band
Joe Witkin - Keyboards
Jocko Marcellino - Drums
Donald 'Donny' York - Vocals
Rob Leonard - Vocals
Alan Cooper - Vocals
Frederick 'Denny' Greene - Vocals
Dave Garrett - Vocals
Richard 'Richie' Joffe - Vocals
Scott Powell - Vocals
Henry Gross - Guitar
Bruce Clarke III - Bass
Elliot Cahn - Rhythm Guitar

JIMI HENDRIX

JIMI HENDRIX WAS very nearly not Woodstock's closing act, and not because the whole thing was over-running to the point where the audience had drastically reduced and of those that were left many must have been exhausted. Those that remained were treated to one of Jimi's most unusual live sets. It was an almost completely different band than the one he had been playing with weeks earlier. It was a very long set, one that included songs Jimi had never played on stage before and didn't ever again. What's perhaps most surprising is the fact that it was under three years since Jimi had become an 'overnight sensation' and here he was topping the bill at Woodstock. The act that Michael Lang wanted to close Woodstock was none other than Roy Rogers, King of the Cowboys, singing 'Happy Trails.' He probably would have left a long time before Jimi and his band.

The boy who was born Johnny Allen Hendrix in November 1942 became known as James Marshall Hendrix a few years later after his father renamed him in honor of his dead brother. Young Johnny had been put into the care of his 17-year-old mother's friends in California, but he was later 'reclaimed' by his father after he left the US Army in which he had served during World War II. Jimi's parents got back together after the war, after which along came four other children, some of whom were put into care and later adopted.

In 1958, Hendrix's mother died and it was around this time that Jimi got his first guitar, the inevitable acoustic, which his father bought from a friend for $5. After seeing him constantly practicing on the acoustic, Hendrix's father bought him his first electric guitar in the summer of '59 – ten years before Woodstock. This white Supro Ozark was what Jimi played in his first band, a group of friends from his home city of Seattle. Apparently, from an early age Jimi was playing the guitar behind his head and with his teeth, as was the way with aspiring R&B guitarists who all wanted to emulate the great tradition of black American electric guitarists that included the brilliant T-Bone Walker and Lonnie Johnson. Jimi also listed and learned from his father's Muddy Waters and B.B. King records.

Apart from his early interest in music, his principal claims to fame as a teenager were getting expelled from school for his poor grades and sloppy attendance, and some run-ins with the law including riding around in stolen cars. He was presented with a choice – prison or the Army – when he came up in court; Jimi chose the U.S. Army and so in May 1961 he headed to Kentucky to join the 101st Airborne Division. A year later, after he showed absolutely

"He was accused of being obscene and was later dropped from a tour of the States with The Monkees when the Daughters of The American Revolution protested that he was corrupting the Daughters' daughters."
~ Chris Welch in Jimi Hendrix's *Melody Maker* obituary

The Jimi Hendrix Experience: Mitch Mitchell, Jimi Hendrix and Noel Redding, 1967

"Man, it's the music, that's what comes first." ~ Jimi Hendrix, March 1968

none of the qualities the army thought a soldier needed, he was discharged. Jimi rarely thereafter mentioned being a soldier, and about his only lasting legacy of his service to his country was his friendship with bass-guitarist Billy Cox, who he met while training.

His first post-army band was the King Kasuals in which Billy Cox played; it also featured another guitarist who apparently played the guitar with his teeth really well; Hendrix quickly learned to do it even better. The band moved to Nashville where they were joined by another guitarist, Larry Lee, and they became the house band at the Club del Morocco. For about two years Hendrix and the Kasuals scraped a living, but in 1964 he decided to try his luck in New York City.

In early 1964 Jimi won a talent contest at Harlem's Apollo Theater, which got him a job in the Isley Brothers' band; they went on tour around the notorious Chitlin' Circuit in the Southern states. Jimi was no stranger to these gigs, having played the venues that were the clubs and juke joints frequented by black people during the post-war period when racial segregation was still rife; it took its name from chitterlings (boiled pig intestines), which were popular throughout the South. He recorded 'Testify' with the Isleys and by the end of the year he had joined Little Richard's band. He recorded with the rock'n'roll pianist and appeared on TV but it seems that neither man liked the other very much, and after a number of 'personality clashes' Jimi left, or more literally 'he missed to bus' one day in Washington; pretty soon he was back playing with the Isleys.

By late 1965 Jimi had met Curtis Knight in a hotel in New York joined his band, The Squires, and somehow wound up touring for a couple of months with Joey Dee and The Starliters, before returning to Knight in October 1965 and playing on a number of Knight's records. Sessions for other people followed before Jimi formed his own band – Jimmy James & The Blue Flames. Among the band was another guitarist, named Randy Wolfe, who Jimi called Randy California on account of their being two Randys in the band – the other Randy came from Texas; Randy California later co-founded Spirit. By early 1966 people were beginning to take notice of Jimmy and the Blue Flames.

Among those who saw Jimi play in New York was Linda Keith, Rolling Stone Keith Richards' girlfriend. She got Andrew Loog Oldham to take a look at them but he wasn't keen on Jimi's music. This was probably in July '66, when the Stones were in New York with Andrew on tour. Next up, Chas Chandler, The Animals' bassist and wannabe manager, took a look and decided Jimi was the man for him, in part because he had a hunch that a song named 'Hey Joe,' written by a guy named Billy Roberts way back in the Fifties, would make a great single.

"You must come and see him – he's great." ~ Chas Chandler, calling a music paper in London, November 1966

Jimi Hendrix (left) with Curtis Knight & The Squires, 1965

Noel Redding, followed by drummer Mitch Mitchell; ironically Mitchell had played with Georgie Fame & The Blue Flames for a while. By the middle of October '66 The Jimi Hendrix Experience were playing their first gigs and had their first hit when 'Hey Joe' made the U.K. charts in January '67.

Jimi appeared all over London, in all the clubs to be seen in, and became a part of the scene; he befriended both Eric Clapton and Pete Townshend. Soon after 'Hey Joe' became a hit, Kit Lambert and Chris Stamp, The Who's managers, signed Jimi to Track Records and it was with that label that he had his second U.K. hit, 'Purple Haze' in March 1967.

This was followed by

Twenty-three-year-old Hendrix arrived in London in the last week of September 1966, having been taken over to Britain from America by Chas Chandler. They set about securing a band and first to sign was bassist

"The Jimi Hendrix Experience are a musical labyrinth – you either find your way into the solid wall of incredible sound, or you sit back and gasp at Hendrix's guitar antics and showmanship, wondering what it's all about." ~ Keith Altham reviewing a gig at Finsbury Park Empire in April 1967, when the Experience appeared on a package tour headlined by Engelbert Humperdink and the Walker Brothers

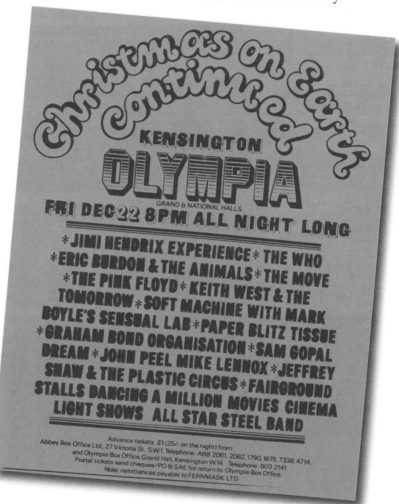

Jimi Hendrix, Eric Burdon and Noel Redding backstage at Olympia, 22 December 1967

Joan Baez and Jimi Hendrix chat between acts at a Biafran Relief Benefit show at Steve Paul's Scene in Manhattan, 29 August 1968

Are You Experienced
(1967)

'The Wind Cries Mary in May,' which heralded his first album – *Are You Experienced*, which was released in late May and made No. 2 in the U.K. charts. After appearing in Europe in late May 1967, Jimi and the Experience flew to California where his set at the Monterey Pop Festival in June did so much to establish his reputation in his homeland. Following Monterey, Reprise released 'Purple Haze' in the U.S.A. and it sauntered up to No. 65 on the charts. This was followed by an American version of the *Are You Experienced* LP, which broke into the top 5 at the end of 1967.

"Our looks may irritate some people, but this is what we look like." ~ Jimi Hendrix

Hendrix was all over the popular press in Britain, causing a sensation as much for his antics on stage and his flamboyant dress as for his music. His next British single was 'Burning of the Midnight Lamp' which got to No. 18 in September followed by a hiatus of a year before his U.K. follow-up, 'All Along

Axis: Bold As Love   (1967)

The Watchtower' came out in October 1968; this made No. 5. Meanwhile back in the U.S.A. 'Foxy Lady' made No. 67 on the *Billboard* chart, followed by 'Up From The Skies' in March 1968, which made No. 82. But Jimi never really was a 'singles' artist concentrating his efforts on

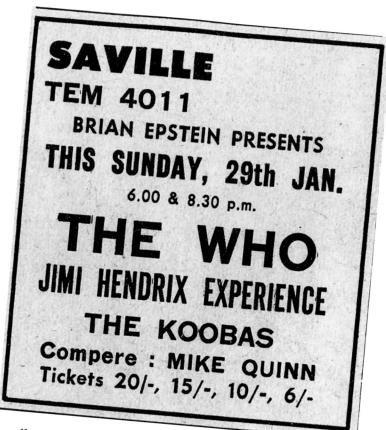

SAVILLE
TEM 4011
BRIAN EPSTEIN PRESENTS
THIS SUNDAY, 29th JAN.
6.00 & 8.30 p.m.
THE WHO
JIMI HENDRIX EXPERIENCE
THE KOOBAS
Compere : MIKE QUINN
Tickets 20/-, 15/-, 10/-, 6/-

albums.

In December 1967 *Axis: Bold As Love* made the U.K. album chart Top 5 and shortly afterwards reached No. 3 on the American equivalent.

'All Along the Watchtower' became Jimi's fourth U.S. hit single in the fall of 1968 when it reached No. 20. It was taken from the third album by the Jimi Hendrix Experience, *Electric Ladyland*, named after the studio in New York where the band recorded this double album, one that is a masterpiece of rock, modern music or indeed any form of music. Such were the circumstances of recording this album, with many of Jimi's friends,

JIMI
HENDRIX
at
SPEAKEASY
Thursday, 19th January
Telephone 580 - 8810
10 p.m.   4 a.m.
Bistro food at bistro prices

Jimi Hendrix performs live at a street concert in Harlem, 9 August 1969, the week before Woodstock

"Man, in this life, you gotta do what you want, you gotta let your mind and fancy flow, flow, flow free."
~ Jimi Hendrix 1968

Electric Ladyland (1968)

'dropping by' the studio that Chas Chandler quit as his manager in May 1968; he found Jimi's requirement for doing take after take just too much to take. Clearly the public didn't care how it was made, and voted their acceptance of the album by taking it to No. 1 in America for two weeks in November '68; in Britain, where Jimi's initial success had been so much greater it made No. 6.

With work on the album finished Jimi moved back to Britain to live, having been in America for most of 1968. He toured Europe and played sold-out shows at London's Royal Albert Hall in February 1969. The Experience then returned to America to record, but things between Noel Redding and Jimi had reached an impasse and following a gig at the Denver Pop Festival on 29 June 1969, Redding quit the band and flew back to London to 'do his own thing' – the wonderfully named, but conversely flat, Fat Mattress.

Jimi had already been jamming with his old army friend Billy Cox, who he had invited to come and stay at the house he was renting near Woodstock. These jams became the basis for the set that Jimi's band would perform at Woodstock. Larry Lee, his old bandmate, had just come back from Vietnam, so he was invited to come along and play too. Two percussionists joined the party and after rehearsing with another drummer, Jimi called Mitch Mitchell to return to the fold to hold the band together for their Woodstock show.

HAROLD DAVISON PRESENTS
AN EVENING WITH
Jimi Hendrix Experience
THE SOFT MACHINE
MASON, CAPALDI
WOOD & FROG
LONDON · ROYAL ALBERT HALL
TUESDAY, 18 FEB., at 7.30 p.m.
TICKETS: 3/6, 7/6, 10/6, 13/6, 16/6, 21/-
Available from ROYAL ALBERT HALL BOX OFFICE (589 8212) and HAROLD DAVISON LTD., REGENT HOUSE, 235-241 REGENT STREET, LONDON, W.1
Please send stamped addressed envelope with postal applications

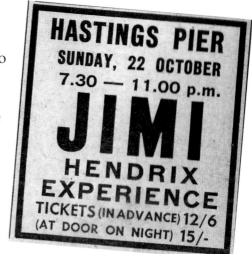

HASTINGS PIER
SUNDAY, 22 OCTOBER
7.30 — 11.00 p.m.
JIMI
HENDRIX
EXPERIENCE
TICKETS (IN ADVANCE) 12/6
(AT DOOR ON NIGHT) 15/-

Jimi Hendrix at the Newport Pop Festival, Northridge, California, 20 June 1969

"It's been a long one, but it's been delightful… Ladies and gentlemen, the Jimi Hendrix Experience." ~ Chip Monck

PERFORMANCE

Mitch Mitchell, Billy Cox and Jimi shared a bottle of Blue Nun wine and then took to the stage for what was one of Jimi's longest-ever shows, running in at over two hours. There were probably something around 150,000 people left in the audience when Jimi and the Band of Gypsies went on early Monday morning. Throughout his set, people were seen to leave and start making their way home by whatever means they could; for some even finding their cars was a challenge.

Besides the tracks and Jimi's appearance in the movie, what we do have of that historic gig is a DVD released in 2005 – *Jimi Hendrix Live at Woodstock*. Many would be forgiven in thinking this was the entire performance as it features all the apparent high spots in the concert; 'Foxy Lady,' 'Fire,' 'Voodoo Child (Slight Return),' 'Purple Haze,' 'Hey Joe,' 'Villanova Junction' and the ubiquitous 'The Star Spangled Banner.' The only problem is, for some reason best known to themselves the Hendrix Estate edited out Larry Lee's songs.

'Mastermind' and 'Gypsy Woman,' the old Curtis Mayfield song, are very good and actually provide a much greater dynamic for the set, breaking up the rapid-fire delivery of Jimi's playing. Jimi understood the dynamics of introducing those songs performed very well by Lee – so why aren't they included?

"We got tired of the Experience; we called it Gypsy Sun and Rainbows, for short it's nothin' but a Band o' Gypsies." ~ Jimi Hendrix

Interestingly, during 'Jam Back at The House' Larry plays a lot of the lead guitar and Jimi plays some brilliant rhythm guitar, but the camera never ever once picks up Larry and exclusively concentrates on Jimi's hands. Also missing is 'Hear My Train A Comin',' which features some great twin lead work by both guitarists.

"You can leave if you want to. We're just jammin." ~ Jimi Hendrix

But what is left on the DVD is still well worth the money and offers a window onto what was a historic set, with some moments of magic. In particular the last 35 minutes or so, which includes the historic 'The Star Spangled Banner' are alone

OVER 120-MINUTE SET

SET LIST
Message to Love
Getting My Heart Back Together Again
Hear My Train a'Coming
Spanish Castle Magic
Red House
Call Me Mastermind
Lover Man
Foxy Lady
Jam Back at The House
Izabella
Gypsy Woman
Fire
Voodoo Child (Slight Return)
Stepping Stone
The Star Spangled Banner
Purple Haze
Woodstock Improvisation
Villanova Junction Blues
Hey Joe

THE BAND
Jimi Hendrix - Guitar, Vocals
Mitch Mitchell - Drums
Billy Cox - Bass
Larry Lee - Rhythm guitar
Juma Sultan - Percussion
Gerardo 'Jerry' Velez - Congas

worth the price. Unsung and overlooked by many is Mitch Mitchell's unique 'lead drum'work. He drives the band along and demonstrates that he too was an integral part of what made Hendrix great; the lack of any decent stage monitors must have made that extremely difficult.

As a postscript to the performance, Jimi's white Fender Stratocaster sold in auction at Sotheby's for $330,660 – a record in 1990. It was sold again in 1993 and now resides in the EMP Museum in Seattle. It's said that it was Bill Gates' right-hand man, Paul Allen, who paid $2 million to take it back to Jimi's birthplace.

"Ladies and gentleman, thank you so VERY much." ~ Chip Monck, the final words from the Woodstock stage

THE WOODSTOCK EFFECT

Did Woodstock make Jimi Hendrix any more famous? Yes and no. His rendition of 'The Star Spangled Banner' did something for his collateral, but given the loose state of affairs with his band he found it difficult to properly move forward. He recorded a live album over New Year's Eve and New Year's Day 1970 with the Band of Gypsies, which was a part settlement of a contract dispute with an old manager. This featured Billy Cox on bass and Buddy Miles on drums.

Immediately afterwards it was announced that the Experience was being brought back together to tour America. In the event, Redding never did get to rehearse or appear and Billy Cox held down the bass gig although Mitch Mitchell returned. This line-up began a U.S. tour in April and it ran through 1 August when it finished in Hawaii. He played the Isle of Wight Festival and the group also spent time in the studio recording tracks that would eventually be released as *The Cry of Love* album.

The Cry of Love (1971)

Some European gigs followed, but Hendrix was not at his best and he finished a concert in Aarhus, Denmark after just two songs. On 6 September he played a festival in Germany, which ended in a small-scale riot; immediately after the gig Billy Cox left and flew home to America. Back in London, on 18 September Jimi Hendrix died at his girlfriend's home under what are still unexplained circumstances. He had taken sleeping tablets before choking on his own vomit.

"When I die, just keep playing the records." ~ Jimi Hendrix

Jimi Hendrix on stage at Woodstock, 18 August 1969

AFTERMATH

"I think these kids are wonderful, but I didn't feel this way prior to the event. I originally entered into this as a business contract but these kids changed my mind." ~ Max Yasgur at the post-festival press conference

IT LOOKED LIKE A DISASTER AREA by the time Woodstock ended; you sank six inches into mud with every step. People had started to leave on Sunday and by Monday the reality of what had happened was beginning to sink in, especially for John Roberts and Joel Rosenman. They got a call from someone at their bank warning them that they needed to be in Manhattan when it opened for a meeting to discuss the huge overdraft they had run up, having written checks for bands who had demanded 'pay or no play.' Midway through their meeting, with seemingly no way out of their mess, they heard that the revenue from the outlets that had been pre-selling tickets looked like topping $2 million. They had been saved from whatever fate the bank had lined up for them.

John Roberts has since claimed that Woodstock Ventures made no money until around 1980 – despite their share of the revenue from album sales as well as movie receipts. As with all such corporate financial activities the devil will be in the detail; without detailed analysis of their accounts who will know the truth of how much was made and by whom at the Aquarian Exposition. Does it even matter?

In the immediate aftermath the press made all sorts of claims. Some were rubbish, but some showed incredible foresight. According to *Time* magazine, "As the moment when the special culture of U.S. youth of the '60s openly displayed its strength, appeal and power, it may well rank as one of the significant political and sociological events of the age."

Interestingly, the press was not so intent on majoring on the magical word – Woodstock. They were just as likely to call it Bethel or Max Yasgur's 600-acre farm. It was after all, a long way from Woodstock.

"The festival turned out to be history's largest happening." ~ *Time* magazine, 29 August 1969

A couple of days after *Time* magazine hit the newsstands, a festival took place at Woodside Bay, near Ryde, on England's Isle Of Wight. Around 150,000 people showed up to see Dylan backed by the Band topping the bill; by all accounts it was a well-run festival. Richie Havens, The Who and Joe Cocker were among the artists that appeared. In 1971 there was anpther Isle of Wight festival, this time 600,000 people saw Jimi Hendrix, The Doors and what seemed like almost every other band in the world. Do people around the world still talk of the Isle of Wight?

There was much more than peace and music at Woodstock – there was magic in the air.

WOODSTOCK, THE SONG

FOR MANY AMERICANS their view of Woodstock was the one through the film-makers lens when the movie debuted in America in March 1970. But for millions more their idea of the Woodstock Festival came from Joni Mitchell's song, the one recorded by Crosby, Stills, Nash & Young that became a hit single.

Joni Mitchell, of course, didn't appear at the festival, her manager at the time encouraged her to appear on *The Dick Cavett Show* from coast to coast on the ABC network; he argued that it was far more prestigious and of more benefit than playing live to a few thousand hippies. Joni at the time was romantically involved with Graham Nash, and while he headed to Bethel she watched events unfold on her TV set stuck in a New York hotel room.

Joni's song got its first public performance at the Big Sur Folk Festival one month after Woodstock, at which Joni appeared along with Crosby, Stills, Nash & Young, Joan Baez and John Sebastian. She subsequently recorded her version for release on her *Ladies Of The Canyon* album in April 1970. In the meantime, boyfriend Nash encouraged his band mates to record their version for their *Déjà Vu* album. They released it as a single in late March, just as the movie was premiering; it eventually rose to No. 11 on the *Billboard* chart.

Across the Atlantic, the film didn't hit cinemas until the summer of 1970 and so Britain was a little slower in getting the 'Woodstock effect.' Encouraged by the success of Crosby, Stills, Nash & Young's version, British band Matthews' Southern Comfort, led by former Fairport Convention vocalist Iain Matthews, decided to record a cover of Joni's song in August 1970. Released in September it went all the way to No. 1 in Britain, staying there for three weeks in November. Whereas Joni's version is stark, with just an electric piano accompaniment, and Crosby, Stills, Nash & Young's version is rock-based, Matthews' Southern Comfort found an interesting middle-ground relying on Gordon Huntley's melodic pedal-steel guitar to give it an almost ethereal quality.

Perhaps more than anything else that set about trying to capture the spirit of Woodstock, including the film and countless articles, Joni's lyrics have created their own mythology. Mentions of 'stardust,' 'golden' people, its anti-war sentiment and the need to get ourselves 'back to the garden' all create a feeling of warmth and a remembrance of a time when all things were possible.

"I liked their performance too in its way. They were seeing Woodstock from the point of view of the performers, while my version is concerned with the spirit of the festival." ~ Joni Mitchell, August 1970

THE ONCE & FUTURE FESTIVAL

WHOEVER IT WAS that coined the phrase 'The Woodstock Nation' created the zeitgeist, while the Baby Boomers in the audience are often referred to as the 'Woodstock Generation.' From the very day that the festival ended until now, and probably forever, we've all been polishing it, perpetuating the myth and reveling in the magic.

"The spontaneous community of youth that was created at Bethel was the stuff of which legends are made; the substance of the event contains both a revelation and a sobering lesson."

~ *Time* magazine, 29 August 1969

"It was not really about the music; it was really all about that decade – it was about the culture."

~ Michael Lang

"On those almost instantly legendary three days there were nearly as many Americans at Woodstock as there were in Vietnam." ~ Writer Greil Marcus

"The whole world was watching us and we had a chance to show the world how it could be if we ran things." ~ Wavy Gravy

"Woodstock, if anything, amounts to the Disneyfication of the entire hippie enterprise – a just-so story about generational togetherness, a sort of temporary '60s theme park that (alas!) has become an annual institution." ~ Writer David Dalton

"Woodstock and Altamont and all the other large-scale things that were characterized by a certain amount of confusion or violence have all produced a new level of paranoia. We still get busted a lot." ~ Jerry Garcia

"All those hippies wandering about thinking the world was going to be different from that day. As a cynical English arsehole I walked through it all and felt like spitting on the lot of them and shaking them and trying to make them realize that nothing had changed and nothing was going to change. Not only that, what they thought was an alternative society was basically a field full of six-foot-deep mud and laced with LSD. If that was the world they wanted to live in, then f*ck the lot of them." ~ Pete Townshend

"It was a nightmare! I wrote a lot of bad paper that weekend. Financially speaking, of course, the festival is a disaster." ~ John Roberts, September 1969

"I can personally guarantee that there will be another Woodstock festival. We'll have a bigger site next time – it's called America." ~ Michael Lang, September 1969

"What happened at Bethel this past weekend was that these young people together with our local residents turned the Aquarian Festival to a dramatic victory for the spirit of peace, goodwill and human kindness." ~ Max Yasgur

WOODSTOCK, THE ALBUMS

Released in America in May 1970 by Atlantic's subsidiary label Cotillion, the triple-album set of the Woodstock Festival was a groundbreaking album and a worldwide best-seller. Entitled *Woodstock: Music from the Original Soundtrack and More*. The 'More' not only refers to the fact that the album contains material not heard in the movie but also because 'Sea of Madness' was recorded in September 1969 at the Fillmore East in New York City.

DISC ONE
Side One
1. 'I Had A Dream' – John Sebastian
2. 'Going Up The Country' – Canned Heat
3. 'Freedom' – Richie Havens
4. 'Rock and Soul Music' – Country Joe & The Fish
5. 'Coming Into Los Angeles' – Arlo Guthrie
6. 'At The Hop' – Sha Na Na

Side Two
1. 'The Fish Cheer'/'I-Feel-Like-I'm-Fixin'-To-Die-Rag' – Country Joe McDonald
2. 'Drug Store Truck Driving Man' – Joan Baez & Jeffrey Shurtleff
3. 'Joe Hill' – Joan Baez
4. 'Suite Judy Blue Eyes' – Crosby, Stills & Nash
5. 'Sea of Madness' – Crosby, Stills, Nash & Young

DISC TWO
Side One
1. 'Wooden Ships' – Crosby, Stills, Nash & Young
2. 'We're Not Gonna Take It' – The Who
3. 'With A Little Help From My Friends' – Joe Cocker

Side Two
1. 'Soul Sacrifice' – Santana
2. I'm Going Home' – Ten Years After

DISC THREE
Side One
1. 'Volunteers' – Jefferson Airplane
2. Medley: 'Dance To The Music'/'Music Lover'/ 'I Want To Take You Higher' – Sly & the Family Stone
3. 'Rainbows All Over Your Blues' – John Sebastian

Side Two
1. 'Love March' – The Paul Butterfield Blues Band
2. Medley: 'The Star Spangled Banner'/'Purple Haze'/'Instrumental Solo' – Jimi Hendrix

ON THE CHARTS
Released 15 August 1970
Woodstock (Cotillion SD3-500 in the U.S.)
Entered the U.S. charts 6 June 1970
Highest position No. 1 (4 weeks)

The Sound Track Album of the Year

WOODSTOCK '69

Coming Soon...
On Cotillion Records & Tapes

Cotillion

Woodstock (Atlantic K60001 in the U.K.)
Entered the U.K. charts 18 July 1970
Highest position No. 35

In 1971 the *Woodstock Two* album was released as a 2-LP set. This had tracks by many of the artists featured on the original album but also included two songs by Melanie ('My Beautiful People' and 'Birthday Of The Sun') along with 'Blood of the Sun' and 'Theme for An Imaginary Western' by Mountain. Neither of the Mountain tracks were recorded at Woodstock, but were captured at some other unknown concert.

DISC ONE
Side One
1. 'Jam Back At The House' – Jimi Hendrix
2. 'Izabella' – Jimi Hendrix
3. 'Get My Heart Back Together' – Jimi Hendrix

Side Two
1. 'Saturday Afternoon'/'Won't You Try'
– Jefferson Airplane
2. 'Eskimo Blue Day' – Jefferson Airplane
3. 'Everything's Gonna Be All Right'
– The Paul Butterfield Blues Band

DISC TWO
Side One
1. 'Sweet Sir Galahad' – Joan Baez
2. 'Guinnevere' – Crosby, Stills, Nash & Young
'3. '4 + 20' – Crosby, Stills, Nash & Young
4. 'Marrakesh Express' – Crosby, Stills, Nash & Young

5. 'My Beautiful People' – Melanie
6. 'Birthday Of The Sun' – Melanie

Side Two
1. 'Blood Of The Sun' – Mountain
2. 'Theme For An Imaginary Western' – Mountain
3. 'Woodstock Boogie' - Canned Heat
4. 'Let The Sunshine In' – Performed by the audience during the rainstorm following Joe Cocker's set

Neither of the Mountain tracks were actually recorded at Woodstock.

ON THE CHARTS
Released 12 July 1971
Woodstock Two (Cotillion SD2-400 in the U.S.)
Entered the U.S. charts 4 October 1971.
Highest position No. 7
Woodstock Two (Atlantic K60002 in the U.K.)
It did not chart in the U.K.

To commemorate the 25th anniversary of Woodstock in 1994 the songs from both albums, as well as numerous additional, previously-unreleased performances from the festival, but not the stage announcements and crowd noises, were reissued on a 4-CD box set titled *Woodstock: Three Days of Peace and Music.*

America's Top 30 LPs

1	(2)	WOODSTOCK	Original Soundtrack, Cotillion
2	(1)	LET IT BE	Beatles, Apple
3	(3)	McCARTNEY	Paul McCartney, Apple
4	(7)	LIVE AT LEEDS	The Who, Decca
5	(15)	SELF PORTRAIT	Bob Dylan, Columbia
6	(5)	ABC	Jackson 5, Motown
7	(9)	DEJA VU	Crosby, Stills, Nash & Young, Atlantic
8	(4)	CHICAGO	Columbia
9	(6)	CANDLES IN THE RAIN	Melanie, Buddah
10	(8)	ON STAGE — FEBRUARY 1970	Elvis Presley, RCA
11	(10)	FIFTH DIMENSION'S GREATEST HITS	Soul City
12	(14)	IT AIN'T EASY	Three Dog Night, Dunhill
13	(—)	BLOOD, SWEAT & TEARS 3	Columbia
14	(16)	THE BEST OF PETER, PAUL & MARY	Warner Bros
15	(26)	CLOSER to HOME	Grand Funks, Capitol
16	(17)	GET READY	Rare Earth, Rare Earth
17	(12)	HENDRIX BAND OF GYPSYS	Jimi Hendrix, Capitol
18	(20)	AMERICAN WOMAN	The Guess Who, RCA
19	(13)	STEPPENWOLF LIVE	Dunhill
20	(18)	THE ISAAC HAYES MOVEMENT	Enterprise
21	(11)	BRIDGE OVER TROUBLED WATER	Simon & Garfunkel, Columbia
22	(22)	STILL WATERS RUN DEEP	Four Tops, Motown
23	(21)	MOUNTAIN CLIMBING	Mountain, Windfall
24	(19)	TOM	Tom Jones, Parrot
25	(23)	BENEFIT	Jethro Tull, Reprise
26	(24)	LIVE CREAM	Atco
27	(40)	WE MADE IT HAPPEN	Engelbert Humperdinck, Parrot
28	(25)	HEY JUDE	Beatles, Apple
29	(27)	THE DEVIL MADE ME BUY THIS DRESS	Flip Wilson, Little David
30	(39)	GASOLINE ALLEY	Rod Stewart, Mercury

WOODSTOCK, THE MOVIE

No one who was there will ever be the same.   Be there.

woodstock 3 days of peace, music...and love

starring joan baez • joe cocker • country joe & the fish • crosby, stills, nash & young • arlo guthrie • richie havens • jimi hendrix • santana • john sebastian • sha-na-na • sly & the family stone • ten years after • the who • and 400,000 other beautiful people

a film by michael wadleigh • produced by bob maurice
a wadleigh-maurice, ltd. production • technicolor® from warner bros.

ANYONE WATCHING the *Woodstock* movie, as millions around the world did in 1970, would probably have had no idea how lucky they were to be able to see it. It almost did not get made for a whole variety of reasons, ranging from the inevitable lack of finance to a lack of interest in the idea of "filming some festival in upstate New York."

John Roberts and Joel Rosenman tried in vain to get a big-name Hollywood movie studio interested in filming the weekend. Movie companies find it easy to say no to ideas and in the case of Woodstock Ventures it was even easier. No-one knew them; they had no track record, and what was so special about their particular festival when compared to all the others taking place that summer? After all, hadn't the *Monterey* film been a dud? Eventually the two entrepreneurs persuaded Michael Wadleigh, who was barely older than they were, but he was a man

gaining a very solid reputation for directing independent films, to take on the task. He had studied to be a neurologist at Columbia Medical School but had opted to spend more time filming mostly gritty documentary subjects with a political bent, shooting two films with Martin Luther King Jr.

Given his age, Wadleigh was a music fan as much as he was a film fan and he saw the opportunities for making documentaries with hard-edged rock soundtracks to complement his multi-screen camera-work and other hip, at the time, camera techniques. Despite Rosenman and Roberts not being in a position to offer any money, Wadleigh felt it was worth a gamble and agreed to film their festival. Such was his dedication to the cause that Wadleigh put up $50,000 of his own money just to buy film stock from Kodak. Wadleigh went up to Woodstock with Martin Scorsese, the 2nd Unit Director, to film and it was through their efforts, their taking a risk, that we have a movie to watch.

Ultimately around 100 people who were on the 'film scene' worked on-site to make the movie happen. Wadleigh didn't have the money to pay them at the time, and buy stock, so he did a unique deal and offered them double or nothing. If the movie took off then they would all get double time, if it failed then they would get zero. All the while, Wadleigh impressed on his camera crews that this was a film about people – hippies and straights – the incomers who had made the pilgrimage and the

"We were all on speed, we virtually did not sleep for four days."
~ Michael Wadleigh

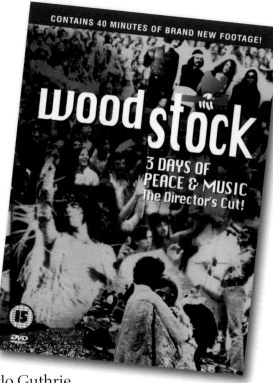

"We had to dub in Sly Stone's organ as his wife had unplugged it, fearful that he would get over-excited while he played and hit the wrong notes." ~ Michael Wadleigh

townspeople who felt threatened by their invasion. It was about the power of people to make a difference and to make something happen. The fact that music happened too was almost secondary to the narrative. It's what makes it work as a film. It's not just a film record of song after song, by an artist or groups, it tells a story of a modern-day *Canterbury Tales*, as Wadleigh told a PBS radio show in 2004.

The 184-minute movie was released in the U.S.A. on 26 March 1970, and having cost in the end $600,00 to produce, it earned $50 million in the U.S. alone. The following year *Woodstock* won an Academy Award as the Best Film Documentary. Since then, Michael Wadleigh has done very little in the way of film work; he admits he became a millionaire from *Woodstock*. His only other work of note was the 1981 film *Wolfen*, starring Albert Finney, which failed to do any serious business at the box office.

Perhaps of greater, lasting, significance is the fact that the *Woodstock* movie is considered 'culturally, historically, or aesthetically significant' by the Library of Congress. In 1994 the 224-minute *Director's Cut* was released on DVD and in 2009 a new version of the *Director's Cut* was released to coincide with the 40th anniversary of three days of love and peace.

ARTIST RUNNING ORDER
'Long Time Gone' – Crosby, Stills & Nash
'Going Up The Country' – Canned Heat
'Wooden Ships' – Crosby, Stills & Nash
'Handsome Johnny' – Richie Havens
'Freedom'/'Sometimes I Feel Like A Motherless Child' – Richie Havens
'A Change Is Gonna Come' – Canned Heat
'Joe Hill' – Joan Baez
'Swing Low, Sweet Chariot' – Joan Baez
'We're Not Gonna Take It'/'See Me, Feel Me' – The Who
'Summertime Blues' – The Who
'At The Hop' – Sha Na Na
'With A Little Help From My Friends' – Joe Cocker
'Rock And Soul Music' – Country Joe & The Fish
'Coming Into Los Angeles' – Arlo Guthrie
'Suite: Judy Blue Eyes' – Crosby, Stills & Nash
'I'm Going Home' – Ten Years After
'Saturday Afternoon'/'Won't You Try' – Jefferson Airplane
'Uncle Sam's Blues' – Jefferson Airplane
'Younger Generation' – John Sebastian
'FISH Cheer'/'I-Feel-Like-I'm-Fixin'-To-Die' Rag – Country Joe McDonald
'Soul Sacrifice' – Santana
'Dance To The Music'/'I Want To Take You Higher' – Sly & The Family Stone
'Work Me, Lord' – Janis Joplin
'Voodoo Chile (Slight Return)' – Jimi Hendrix
'The Star Spangled Banner' – Jimi Hendrix
'Purple Haze' – Jim Hendrix
'Woodstock Improvisation' – Jimi Hendrix
'Villanova Junction' – Jimi Hendrix
'Woodstock'/'Find the Cost of Freedom' – Crosby, Stills & Nash

WOODSTOCK 94

ANNIVERSARIES ARE AS OFTEN as not a good time to remember past glories and so the 25th anniversary of Woodstock – 3 Days of Peace & Music was honored with Woodstock 94 – 2 More Days of Peace & Music. Rather cunningly the poster of the event, while replicating the original, had two doves perched on the neck of the guitar. When it finally came down to it, all the marketing was slightly undermined when a third day, 12 August, was added to the two-day festival that took place over the weekend of 13 and 14 August.

The site chosen for this 1994 burst of déjà-vu was at Saugerties, 10 miles from Woodstock (100 miles from New York City), and it was at one time the site proposed for the 1969 festival before it got moved to Max Yasgur's farm. Arguably, from a geographical standpoint, this really was a Woodstock Festival.

popularity had only been established in the previous decade, but there were a few other performers who could, given different circumstances, have been on stage at the original festival. Most notable was Bob Dylan, who topped the bill on the Sunday and whose set was considered to be outstanding by all the critics that saw him; this despite him being 90 minutes late on stage, which at least proved how much things had improved in the time-keeping department over the previous 25 years. Neil Young turned down $1 million to appear.

Todd Rundgren was also present, as were Traffic, who were in the middle of a one-off reunion tour; of the original line-up only Steve Winwood and drummer Jim Capaldi were with them. Veteran rockers the Allman Brothers with Gregg Allman, Dickey Betts, Butch Trucks and Jai Johanny Johanson

"We waited 25 years to hear this. Ladies and gentlemen, Mr Bob Dylan."
~ The announcement heralding the arrival onstage of Dylan

Among the performers at Woodstock 94 there were a few survivors from the original festival. The Band were there, although without Robbie Robertson or the late Richard Manuel, but they did have Bob Weir on guitar who had played with the Dead in 1969; both Jorma Kaukonen and the bassist Jack Casady, who were with Jefferson Airplane sat, in with them. Joe Cocker performed, as did Country Joe McDonald and John Sebastian. Crosby, Stills & Nash along with Santana were the only other two bands to appear at both festivals.

Many of the other bands were young bands whose

from the original band were also in attendance. Paul Rodgers of Bad Company played the event accompanied by Slash from Guns 'N' Roses and Neil Schon on guitars, along with Jason Bonham on drums. Among the songs he played was 'Feel Like Making Love,' which was one of the themes of Woodstock 94

Among the modern bands were James, Scottish rockers Del Amitri, Sheryl Crow, The Cranberries, Metallica, Nine Inch Nails, Green Day, Peter Gabriel, and the Red Hot Chilli Peppers. Aerosmith played their part; apparently Steve Tyler and Joey Kramer had been in the audience of the original festival. They no doubt appreciated the much-improved organization behind Woodstock 94, at least as far as the bands were concerned.

"The Cranberries, an Irish folk-rock band, paid homage to one of the next generation's guilty pleasures by performing The Carpenters' hit 'Close to You'."
~ *The New York Times*

Just like at the original festival mud, was a key feature after a deluge on the Saturday; during Green Day's set on the Sunday a mud fight developed. It culminated with Mike Dirnt, their bass player, being mistaken for a mud-covered member of the audience. He was apparently manhandled by a security guard, which resulted in the Green Day man losing several teeth. Nevertheless, their performance is considered by many to be one of the outstanding sets of the entire weekend.

"This time the revolution is televised." ~ *Boston Globe* headline, 15 August 1994

Mud was one of the overriding themes of the event, to the point where people even began calling it 'Mudstock.' This was much in evidence in the 1995 movie *Woodstock 94* which, like its predecessor, set out to capture the performers and try to give something of an all-round view of the weekend's happenings.

The event, the movie and just about everything associated with Woodstock 2, barring a few notable exceptions, was seen by fans and commentators alike to be the ultimate embodiment of the over-the-counter culture. Tickets for the two-day event were priced at $135 when bought through Ticketron outlets – the original Woodstock three-day ticket was priced at $72 at 1994 prices. Yes, it was on television in America thanks to a PolyGram Diversified Ventures pay-per-view service costing $49.95 for Saturday and Sunday's line-ups. Arguably marketing was pre-eminent and the music secondary.

Just like the first Woodstock, similar problems beset the 1994 show when, after selling around 200,000 tickets, they ran out of car parking space and eventually ended up letting people in for nothing. However, despite what commentators called the Woodstock 'rule fest' nature had the last laugh by sending the vast crowd home a lot more bedraggled than when they arrived. Some things definitely don't change.

Still, you have to ask yourself, what happened to the dream?…

Stephen Stills, Graham Nash and David Crosby get themselves back to the garden, 13 August 1994

INDEX

A

Aldergrove Beach Rock Festival, 14, 20
Alpert, Richard, 25
Altamont Festival, 10, 162
Altham, Keith, 226
Anderson, Miller, 100-101
Andrew, Sam, 135-137, 139
Animals, The 224
Artwoods, The, 100
Atlanta Pop Festival, 15, 21
Atlantic City Pop Festival, 15, 21

B

Baker, Ginger, 115
Baez, Joan, 16-17, 50, 56, 63, **78-81**, 228, 229
Balin, Marty, 158-163
Band, The, 50, 56, 81, **186-191**, 215
Bath Festival, 15, 21
Beach Boys, The, 100
Beatles, The, 28-29, 69, 170-171, 173
Berry, Chuck, 15, 109
Bethel, 8, 36-37, 41
Big Brother & the Holding Company, 25, 30-31, 135 -137, 139, 176
Big Sur Folk Festival, 229
Blind Faith, 14, 206
Blood, Sweat & Tears, 15, 50, 56, **200-203**
Bloomfield, Mike, 93, 94, 214
Bowen, Michael, 22-23, 24-25
Brown, Pete, 116
Bruce, Jack, 115-117
Buffalo Springfield, 209
Burdon, Eric, 227
Butterfield, Paul Blues Band, The, 50, 65, 129, **214-215**
Byrds, The, 14, 15, 80, 191, 206, 209

C

Canned Heat, 8, 50, 56, **108-111**
Casady, Jack, (Jefferson Airplane), 45, 158-163
Cass, Mama, 209
Chambers Brothers, The, 14
Changin' Times, The, 32
Chicken Shack, 15
Clapton, Eric, 69, 115, 191, 226
Collins, Albert, 15

Country Joe & The Fish, 14, 50, 56, **89**, **176-177**
Cocker, Joe, 15, 50, 56, **170-173**, 250
Cox, Billy, 232, 235
Cream, 115- 117
Creedence Clearwater Revival, 15, 50, 51, 56, **128-131**
Crosby, David, 45, 163
Crosby, Stills, Nash & Young, 52, 56, **206-211**, 239, 250, 252-253
Crumb, Robert, 136
Crusaders, The, 173

D

Davis, Spencer, 101
Deep Purple, 100, 191
Denver Pop Festival, 21, 232
Derringer, Rick, 196-197
Diddley, Bo, 15
Doors, The, 14, 15, 29, 120, 238
Dylan, Bob, 63, 78-81, 130, 171, 186-191, 197, 238, 250

E

Electric Flag, 14
Ertegun, Ahmet, 73
Even Dozen Jug Band, The, 98

F

Fairport Convention, 239
Family, 15
Fantasy Faire & Magic Mountain Music Festival, 12, 19
Farina, Mimi, 16-17, 80
Farina, Richard, 80
Fleetwood Mac, 15, 100, 129
Flock, 15
Fogerty, John, (Creedence Clearwater Revival), 46

G

Garcia, Jerry, 44, 120-125, 163, 243
Ginsberg, Alan, 22-23, 25
Glass, Philip, 69
Graham, Bill, 93, 94
Graham Central Station, 143
Grateful Dead, The, 14, 25, 52, 56, **120-125**, 129, 135, 191
Greer, Maretta, 22-23
Grisman, David, 98
Guitar Shorty, 14
Guthrie, Arlo, 52, 56, **74-75**
Guthrie, Woody, 74
Guy, Buddy, 139

H

Haggard, Merle, 124
Haight-Ashbury, 25
Hardin, Tim, 52, 56, **66-67**, 115
Harper, Roy, 14
Harrison, George, 26-27, 69, 130
Hartley, Keef, 15, 52, 56, **100-101**
Havens, Richie, 14, 15, 41, 44, 52, 56, **62-63**
Hawkins Singers, The Edwin, 73
Hawkins, Ronnie, 186
Hendrix, Jimi (Experience), 14, 15, 25, 28-29, 46, 52, 53, 56, 116, **222-237**, 238
Hoffman, Abbie, 27, 45, 152
Hog Farmers Collective, The, 36, 38-39
Hollies, The, 206, 209
Hooker, John Lee, 181
Hopper, Dennis, 29
Hot Tuna, 162
Howlin' Wolf, 93, 214
Human Be-In, 24, 29, 161
Hyde Park concerts, 14, 15, 20, 21, 63

I

Incredible String Band, The, 52, 56, 98, **104-105**
Isle of Wight Festival, 14, 20, 189, 238

J

Jefferson Airplane, 12, 14, 15, 52, 56, 120, 129, 135, **158-163**, 250
Jefferson Starship, 163
Jethro Tull, 14, 129
Jones, Brian, 25, 28
Joplin, Janis, 14, 30-31, 52, 56, **134-139**, 163, 191

K

Kantner, Paul, (Jefferson Airplane), 46, 158-163

Kaukonen, Jorma, (Jefferson Airplane), 45, 135, 158-163
King, Albert, 15
Knight, Curtis & The Squires, 225
Kooper, Al, 94, 188, 200-201, 214
Kornfield, Arthur (Artie), 32-33, 36-37, 45, 65

L

Laing, Laurence 'Corky', 117, 183
Lang, Michael, 32-37, 44, 47, 63, 218, 222, 242, 243
Leary, Timothy, 25
Led Zeppelin, 15
Lee, Albert, 171
Left Banke, 65
Lewis, Jerry Lee, 109
Little Richard, 15, 224
Love, 15
Lovin' Spoonful, The, 97

M

Mamas & The Papas, The, 14, 25, 64
Marcus, Greil, 242, 210
Matthews Southern Comfort, 239
Mayall, John, 15, 100
McCartney, Paul, 69, 105
McDonald, Country Joe, 14, 50, 56, **89**, **176-177**
McLaughlin, John, 95
McCullough, Henr,y 171
McCoys, The, 197
Melenie (Safka), 41, 52, 56, **72-73**
Menuhin, Yehudi, 69
Miller, Steve, 120
Mitchell, Joni, 15, 239
Moby Grape, 158
Monck, Chip, 188, 235, 236
Monkees, Th,e 109
Monterey Pop Festival, 12, 19, 26, 28-29, 109, 135, 176, 229
Mountain, 54, 56, **114-117**
Mugwumps, The, 98

N

National Jazz & Blues Festival, 12, 18, 19, 20, 21
Neil, Fred, 115
Nevins, Nancy, (Sweetwater) 44, 64
New Vaudeville Band, The, 14
Newport Folk Festival, 15, 18, 19, 20, 21
Newport Jazz Festival, 12, 18
Newport Pop Festival, 14, 20
Newport '69, 15, 20
Nice, The, 15

P

Page, Jimmy, 171
Pappalardi, Felix, (Mountain), 114-117
Paxton, Tom, 115
Pennebaker, D.A., 28
Pentangle, 15
Pink Floyd, 14
Plumpton, 15
Poco, 15
Pomeroy, Wes, 44
Presley, Elvis, 180, 194
Preston, Billy, 173
Procol Harum, 15

Q

Quicksilver Messenger Service, 14, 25, 120, 163, 176
Quill, 54, 56, **88**

R

Rascals, The, 15
Redding, Otis, 14, 25
Roberts, John, 32-37, 41, 238, 243, 248
Robinson, Smokey, 14
Rolling Stones, The, 10, 15, 19, 25, 64, 73, 100, 123, 162, 194, 224
Rosenman, Joel, 32-37, 41, 238, 248
Russell, Leon, 173

S

Saint-Marie, Buffy, 115
San Francisco, 24-25
Santana, 15, 45, 54, 56, **92-95**, 250
Satchidananda, His Holiness Sri Swami, 58-59
Satriani, Joe, 117
Scorsese, Martin, 125, 191, 248
Seattle Pop Festival, 21
Sebastian, John, 44, 54, 56, **98-99**, 229, 250
Seeger, Pete, 74
Sha Na Na, 54, 56, **218-219**
Shankar, Ravi, 14, 54, **68-69**
Shorter, Wayne, 95
Skolnick, Arnold, 33
Slick, Grace, (Jefferson Airplane), 46, 141, 158-163
Sommer, Bert, 54, 56, **65**
Sonny & Cher, 14
Spanky & Our Gang, 64
Spence, Skip, 158
Spirit, 15, 109, 224
Stainton, Chris, 170-173
Stanley, Owsley, 25, 124
Starr, Ringo, 100, 155

Status Quo, 130
Steppenwolf, 15
Stone, Sly (and the Family Stone), 47, 54, 56, **140-143**
Sweetwater, 54, 56, **64**
Synder, Gary, 22-23, 25

T

Taj Mahal, 129, 194
Taylor, Derek, 25, 26-27
Taylor, James 15
Ten Wheel Drive, 15
Ten Years After, 54, 56, **180-183**
Three Dog Night, 15
Tiber, Elliot, 36-37
Tiny Tim, 14, 186
Toronto Festival, 21
Turner, Tina, 130
Tyrannosaurus Rex, (T. Rex), 14, 101

U

Uriah Heep, 101

V

Visconti, Tony, 170

W

Wadleigh, Michael, 36-37, 248-249
Wallkill, 8, 33
Warnes, Jennifer, 173
Warwick, Dionne, 14
Waters, Muddy, 18, 191, 214, 222
Wavy Gravy, 36-37, 38-39, 46, 242
West, Leslie, 114-117
Who, The, 14, 15, 25, 54, 55, 56, 57, 95, **146-155**, 226, 229, 238
Williamson, Sonny Boy, 183
Winter, Edgar, 196
Winter, Johnny, 15, 54, 56, **194-197**
Woburn Festival, 14. 20
Wolff, John, 146
Woodstock Ventures, 32-33, 36-37, 41, 73, 238
Wyman, Bill, 196

Y

Yasgur, Max, 8, 36-37, 238, 243, 250
Yes, 15
Young, Neil, 191

THANKS & RESOURCES

Like us, if you weren't there you have to rely on the testimony of others and the resources provided by the web, as well as books, magazines and newspapers.

Lots of people have helped in putting this book together; they came up with advice, insights, contacts and tips. They include: Sam Andrew (Big Brother & the Holding Company), Kit Buckler, Mick Brown, Paul Conroy, Dave Crowe, Tina Chase Gillmor, Chris Haralambous, Victor Khan, Phil Beards, John Morawski, Al Kooper, Paul Moreton, Andy Neill, Tony Robinson, Ethan Russell, Tony Visconti and Bill Wyman. A big thank you to Shelley Faye Lazar for her creative skills; Christine Havers for her photography and to both of them for their support.

THE WEB

Numerous websites about the artists who appeared, both official and unofficial, were consulted. A lot of the time it just goes to prove how little people really remember. The principal online resources were:
• Wikipedia is, as ever, an invaluable tool. Why not make a financial contribution next time you use it!
• www.woodstock69.com – As they say, "A collection of Woodstock Facts, Figures, Stories, Photos, Current Happenings, Memorabilia, Links, and Assorted Tidbits."
• www.rocksbackpages.com – A fantastic resource for reading and researching all things rock
• www.highbeam.com – An online library of 3,500 publications including newspapers and magazines
• www.marmalade-skies.co.uk – The home of British psychedelia
• www.ukrockfestivals.com – The Archive: A history of British rock festivals
• www.pappalardi.com – Everything you'd ever need to know about the late Felix Pappalardi

BOOKS & MAGAZINES

Hippie by Miles (Octopus Publishing), *The Billboard Book of Top 40 Albums* (Billboard Publications), *The Billboard Book of Top Pop Singles* (Record Research Inc.), *The Complete Book of the British Charts* (Omnibus Press), *Stand & Be Counted* by David Crosby & David Bender (Harper San Francisco), *Summer of Love* by Joel Selvin (Dutton Books), *The Grateful Dead – The Illustrated Trip* (Dorling Kindersley), *Anyway Anyhow Anywhere – The Complete Chronicles of The Who* by Andy Neill & Matt Kent (Friedman/Fairfax Publishing), *The Jefferson Airplane and The San Francisco Sound* by Ralph Gleason (Ballantine Books) and *Tony Visconti – The Autobiography* by Tony Visconti & Richard Havers (Harper Collins). Countless copies of *Melody Maker*, *Disc & Music Echo*, *The New Musical Express*, *Crawdaddy*, *Record Mirror* and *Mojo* plus CD liner notes far too numerous to mention.

"This is my truth, tell me yours."
~ Aneurin Bevan

Richard Havers & Richard Evans
January 2009